THOMAS SHOTTER BOYS

THOMAS SHOTTER BOYS

1803-1874

by
James Roundell

Foreword by Malcolm Horsman – Introduction by Alastair Smart

Octopus Books

ACKNOWLEDGMENTS

We owe an overwhelming debt of thanks to Mrs Rosemary Tailby for her untiring research, and for the lengthy task of typing out the manuscript. We owe gratitude to Miss Jane Pickard for making valuable suggestions about the manuscript and for her constant advice right from the book's inception. We must record our debt to the staffs of museums in England, America and France, and to the members of the art trade, in particular Mr Bill Thomson of the Albany Gallery and Mr Anthony Reed of the Manning Gallery, for their generous assistance. We would also like to thank Dr Marion Spencer for her frequent suggestions about the relationship between Bonington and Boys. Our thanks also to Professor Smart for agreeing to write the introduction at rather short notice; and to Christie's for their kind co-operation. We must also record our thanks to all the many people who have been so liberal in their help, but who are too numerous to list. In particular, we would like to extend our thanks to all the owners and curators who have kindly given permission for us to illustrate pictures in their collections. Finally, we are grateful to Mr Michael Leitch for his invaluable editorial advice, and to Octopus Books for producing the book in time for Boys's centenary exhibition at the Nottingham University Gallery and at Agnew's, London.

James Roundell
Malcolm Horsman

First published 1974 by
Octopus Books Limited
59 Grosvenor Street, London W1

ISBN 0 7064 0388 6

Made and printed in Great Britain by
William Clowes & Sons, Limited, London, Beccles and Colchester

CONTENTS

FOREWORD

by Malcolm Horsman

THE year 1974 marks the centenary of the death of Thomas Shotter Boys. He died, as he had lived his last thirty years, in obscurity. He is buried in Islington Cemetery, close to the area where he spent most of his mature life. Very little is known about the artist himself. One possible reason is that he died childless (many famous artists owe their eminence not only to their output but also to the attention drawn to them by their children).

As a collector of watercolours, I became particularly attracted to Boys's work at an early stage. The spontaneity and freshness of his drawing, especially around the 1830s, and also his later lithographic work conveyed the feeling that here was an artist who deserved far more appreciation than he has had in the past. It is astonishing that nothing of any note has been written on Boys except for an article by Hugh Stokes in *Walker's Quarterly* in 1926; otherwise every comment, either written or verbal, has merely repeated the invidious comparison between him and Richard Parkes Bonington.

In the summer of 1973, I heard through a friend that a Cambridge undergraduate was doing research on Boys. In September we met and decided to pool our resources to produce a book which would re-assess this Victorian artist on several fronts—one being his relationship with Bonington and another his unique contribution to lithography; we felt, too, that the act of bringing together and illustrating a wide selection of his work would in itself clearly demonstrate his skills.

It is hard to believe that, while examples from the *London as it is* series of lithographs are found in almost every other house or office in London, so little acknowledgment has been accorded to the man who produced them. They have a quite outstanding charm and an empathy for their subject which have given them a current popularity similar to that enjoyed by the prints of Piranesi and works by the Impressionists.

Like most nineteenth-century topographical watercolourists, Boys was primarily interested in depicting European architectural scenes or rustic landscapes; but in *London as it is* he went a long way towards conveying sympathetically the ordinary life of the city. The road mender, the delivery boy, the street vendor—all are shown clearly as integral parts of the life of the times. This is what makes the lithographs so fascinating to people today.

Although Boys was clearly observant and generally aware of all things around him, it is strange to think that someone who was an adolescent in Napoleonic times, and spent a good deal of his early working life in Paris, a city filled with ferment and danger, and who grew up in England at a time of industrial revolution and colonial conquest, should produce only one known watercolour reflecting contemporary history—his *View of Brussels* of 1830 showing a battle-scarred town with soldiers in the street.

James Roundell has explored Boys's relationship with Bonington in detail and, I believe, has now established beyond doubt that Boys was not just a docile follower of Bonington but in many cases produced work of a greater quality. As the text makes clear, Boys and Bonington were two young artists in a foreign city, very close in age, who worked happily together to the artistic benefit of both. Bonington's tragic death in romantic circumstances, however, had the effect of highlighting his great skills as an artist; and at the same time this tended to obliterate any reputation which Boys might have gained from his own early watercolours.

Boys's pictures are found in museums and galleries on both sides of the Atlantic. I concentrated on viewing his works in North American collections, whilst James Roundell investigated those in the United Kingdom and France. I believe that the illustrations that we have presented here will help to increase the general awareness of Boys's achievements. I also feel that the detailed analysis that James Roundell has made of Boys's lithographic technique and his inventiveness in the field of chromolithography will surprise many readers and bring out a side of his activities that hitherto has been largely ignored.

It is my hope that this book will not only enable the reader to assess Thomas Shotter Boys in a new and clearer light but, at the same time, will give considerable visual pleasure.

March 1974

LIST OF ILLUSTRATIONS

All illustrations are by Thomas Shotter Boys unless otherwise stated.

Jacket: Detail from *The Tower and Mint, from Great Tower Hill*, Plate III in *London as it is*, published in London, 1842.

Frontispiece: *Pavillon de Flore, Paris*, watercolour, $13\frac{3}{8} \times 10\frac{3}{8}$ ins/340 × 263 mm., signed (BR) *T. Boys/1829*, Victoria and Albert Museum, London (AL 5745). Crown copyright reserved.

Title-page vignette: Detail from the portrait of Thomas Shotter Boys and E. W. Cooke, oil painting, artist unknown, Private Collection, England.

INTRODUCTION
by Alastair Smart

IF he had produced nothing else but the volume of lithographs published in 1842 under the title *Original Views of London as it is,* Thomas Shotter Boys would claim our attention as a national figure worthy of comparison with any other of the great masters of the English topographical tradition. Whether we compare him with such predecessors as Paul Sandby and Thomas Rowlandson, or whether we consider him in relation to his contemporaries, among whom the names of Samuel Prout, R.P. Bonington and J.D. Harding come particularly to mind, his individuality and indeed originality stand out with the utmost clarity, both in his innovatory work in lithography and in his attainments as one of the finest watercolourists of his age. It is surprising, therefore, that he should have been so neglected by historians of English art.

Such writers as Felix Man and Michael Twyman have reminded us of Boys's importance in the history of lithography; and in the sensitive pages of Martin Hardie he appears as a distinguished exponent of Bonington's method as a watercolourist: but until now there has been only one monograph on Boys—the brief but commendable study published by Hugh Stokes in 1926. A more complete account of Boys's art has long been needed; and the publication, on the centenary of the artist's death, of James Roundell's investigations, coinciding with an exhibition in the Nottingham University Art Gallery and at Agnew's in London, offers a welcome addition to the literature. Even apart from his position in the history of lithography, Boys will emerge, I am sure, as much more than an able follower of Bonington, as indeed Stokes himself predicted when he wrote:

> The delicacy and atmospheric value of his watercolours must ultimately give him a far higher place in the annals of the English school than he has hitherto occupied. He is assuredly one of the Little Masters.

The reasons for Boys's neglect appear to have their roots in the obscure circumstances of his life. Although we lack the materials for a complete inquiry, the question is an intriguing one and is worth exploring, not least because it bears upon the larger question of his relationship to his precursors and contemporaries and of his place in the great English school of watercolour. I think that at the very beginning we are faced with a paradox. Before the appearance of *London as it is,* Boys had established a considerable reputation with his *Picturesque Architecture in Paris, Ghent, Antwerp, Rouen etc,* published in 1839 in collaboration with the printer Charles Hullmandel. The importance of this work can be judged from Felix Man's account of it in his Introduction to the catalogue of the exhibition *Homage to Senefelder,* which was held in 1971 at the Victoria and Albert Museum:

> This album, printed in colour from a series of stones, not coloured by hand, represents a decisive breakthrough in the field of artists' colour lithography. The colours were printed directly as flat tints and were not produced by overprinting. It was not until years later during the renaissance of artists' lithography in France, stemming from the posters of Chéret, Toulouse-Lautrec and Bonnard, that this use of colour in lithography was established as an expressive medium.

Then, three years afterwards, in *London as it is,* Boys not only created a unique interpretation of the character and life of the metropolis, but made a further, important advance in lithographic technique: he departed from the practice of his contemporaries in his recognition of the potentialities of lithography as a medium in its own right, and was no longer concerned with the mere imitation of the characteristics of watercolour. The emphasis placed by James Roundell upon Boys's historical importance as the true inventor of chromolithography draws attention to an achievement to which *London as it is*, in tinted lithography, was the crowning monument. Yet as we attempt to penetrate the obscurities of Boys's career after 1842, that monument begins to take on the appearance of a tomb: after 1842 the rising flame of Boys's high reputation flickers and falters as other men, as it seems, supplant him in public favour and esteem. Financial difficulties may well have placed insuperable obstacles in the way of his career as a lithographer: but perhaps the most interesting question concerns the apparent decline of his reputation as a watercolourist. He never, for example, achieved the success enjoyed by William Callow, an artist indebted to him and comparable with him in many ways although much inferior to him.

One solution to the problem was suggested by Stokes when he pointed out that Ruskin, while enlisting Boys's services as an etcher for *Modern Painters* and *The Stones of Venice,* never wrote anything about his art, beyond commending his 'fidelity' in the journeyman's labour upon which he had employed him. Ruskin's neglect of Boys in his critical writings is indeed curious, and, as Stokes observed, 'his word was law to the wealthy collectors of the 'fifties and 'sixties. The word was not given, and Thomas Shotter Boys passed slowly into oblivion.' Stokes's hypothesis is worth pursuing in more detail, and there may well be much truth in his further observation that, since Ruskin was unsympathetic to the work of Bonington, Boys's early association with Bonington in Paris and his general indebtedness to his style would not, in Ruskin's eyes, have been to his advantage.

Although Ruskin was a very young man when he wrote the first volume of *Modern Painters,* he was well acquainted with recent developments in English watercolour painting: he had, at an early age, been taught the techniques of watercolour by Copley Fielding, whom, together with J. D. Harding, he regarded as one of his two principal masters. He knew, besides, the work of Samuel Prout, whose topographical drawings and lithographs may be said to have prepared the way for those by Boys, David Roberts and other artists of the period. Indeed at the very moment when Boys was beginning work on *London as it is,* Ruskin was in Italy making, as he wrote many years later, 'a series of pencil sketches, partly in imitation of Prout, partly of David Roberts'. Ruskin must have been familiar with Boys's *Picturesque Architecture* of 1839, and the first volume of *Modern Painters* was published in May 1843, about a year after the appearance of *London as it is*; we know that Ruskin was still at work on the volume in the winter of 1842–43, and yet, while devoting particular attention to the topographical work of Prout in both watercolour and lithography, neither this nor any subsequent volume of *Modern Painters* contains even the barest reference to the already celebrated achievements of Boys in the same tradition.

On the other hand the ardent young author was able to mention Prout in the same breath with Leonardo and Raphael. Above all, Ruskin observed in Prout the expression of a new sensibility, that taste for the accidental effects of weathering and time upon old buildings which so much appealed to the Victorians:

> We owe to Prout, I believe, the first perception, and certainly the only existing expression, of precisely the characters which were wanting to old art; of that feeling which results from the influence, among the noble lines of architecture, of the rent and the rust, the fissure, the lichen, and the weed, and from the writing upon the pages of ancient walls of the confused hieroglyphics of human history. I suppose, from the deserved popularity of the artist, that the strange pleasure which I find myself in the deciphering of these is common to many. The feeling has been rashly and thoughtlessly contemned as mere love of the picturesque; there is, as I have above shown, a deeper

moral in it, and we owe much, I am not prepared to say how much, to the artist by whom pre-eminently it has been excited: for, numerous as have been his imitators, extended as his influence, and simple as his means and manner, there has yet appeared nothing at all to equal him; there is *no* stone drawing, *no* vitality of architecture like Prout's. I say not this rashly: I remember Mackenzie and Haghe, and many other capital imitators; and I have carefully reviewed the architectural work of the Academicians, often most accurate and elaborate. I repeat there is nothing but the work of Prout which is true, living, or right, in its general impression, and nothing, therefore, so inexhaustibly agreeable.

After praising the excellence of Prout's lithographic work, and especially of the views in Flanders and Germany, Ruskin draws attention to the artist's skill in introducing appropriate figures into his compositions:

It is not, however, only by his peculiar stone touch, nor by his perception of human character, that he is distinguished. He is the most dexterous of all our artists in a certain kind of composition. No one can place figures as he can, except Turner. It is one thing to know where a piece of blue or white is wanted, and another to make the wearer of the blue apron or white cap come there, and not look as if it were against her will. Prout's streets are the only streets that are accidentally crowded; his markets the only markets where one feels inclined to get out of the way. With others we feel the figures so right where they are, that we have no expectation of their going anywhere else; and approve of the position of the man with the wheelbarrow, without the slightest fear of his running it against our legs.

It would be possible to read into this trenchant appreciation of the busy, bustling pencil of Prout an implicit criticism of the quieter and carefully ordered world of Boys's more contemplative vision. The vitality and imagination of Prout's genius naturally appealed to Ruskin's romantic temperament: but there lies at the heart of Boys's approach to the selfsame subject-matter an essential 'classicism', if I may so term it, in which ordered clarification takes precedence over accidental incident, and in which the momentary impression is modified by a sense of time-lessness. Whether or not Ruskin was thinking of Boys in particular when he contrasted the work of Prout with that of his 'imitators', he had no hesitation in dismissing almost all of them, although he allowed that there was merit in Haghe's 'fidelity' (the same adjective that he was to apply in 1856 to Boys's etchings for the fourth volume of *Modern Painters*) and in Joseph Nash's popular illustrations of the architecture of the Middle Ages. As Ruskin put it:

Many other dexterous and agreeable architectural artists we have, of various degrees of merit, but all of whom, it may be generally said, that they draw hats, faces, cloaks and caps much better than Prout, but *figures* not so well: that they draw walls and windows, but not cities; mouldings and buttresses, but not cathedrals.

Such criticisms could certainly have been applied by Ruskin's readers to Boys, whose figures lack the vigour of Prout's but are so charming in the exquisiteness of the touching in of their attire, and whose treatment of architectural detail is less bold than Prout's but at the same time far more refined. And with this passage in *Modern Painters* in mind, it is worth remarking that the colour notes in the costumes of Boys's figures usually play a vital role in the total colour-orchestration of his compositions, and must have been carefully calculated; and, further, that it was surely one of Boys's most remarkable achievements that he was able, in his representations of buildings, to combine the finest precision of detail with a general effect of unity.

Boys is rarely dramatic, as Prout often is; and at times—as, for example, in the lovely, pellucid *Notre-Dame, Paris, from the Quai St-Bernard* (from the *Picturesque Architecture* of 1839: see Plate 60) —the measured clarity of his art recalls the best work of Cotman, and possesses a comparable quality of still 'quietism'. In another sense also the ethos of Boys's art was different from that of Prout's; for whereas Prout, who was born in 1783 and was therefore Boys's senior by twenty years, belongs essentially to the Romantic Age, most of Boys's major works were executed during the reign of Queen Victoria and reflect a subtle change in taste, notwithstanding the origins of his lithographic and watercolour style in the circle of Bonington and Francia. Prout had been appointed painter in watercolours to George IV, and although he was retained in this office by Queen Victoria (up to his death in 1852), he had long since established his reputation as the most eminent topographical artist of the period. That reputation must have been enhanced by Ruskin's eulogies; and by the same token the less assertive genius of Boys, despite the immediate success of his two great series of lithographs, may well have been overshadowed by it.

Similarly, other artists praised by Ruskin, such as David Roberts (born in 1796) and J.D. Harding (born in 1797), who can be regarded as rivals of Boys, also made their reputations earlier, and sustained them throughout their careers: Harding, a pupil of Prout's, became famous for his manuals on landscape drawing, which enjoyed a wide vogue; and Roberts, by his *Picturesque Sketches in Spain* of 1837 and his *Sketches in the Holy Land, Syria, Idumea, Arabia, Egypt and Nubia,* published in four volumes in 1855–56, appealed to a new taste for exotic subjects in landscape which evidently lay outside Boys's interests. This last factor, which is epitomized by the Egyptian scenes of John Frederick Lewis, with their romanticized glimpses of the mysteries of the harem, may well provide us with one of the most significant clues to the reasons for Boys's decline, in later life, into relative obscurity. The excitements offered by the exploration by numerous English artists of the countries of the Middle East, in which the religious appeal of depictions of the Holy Land played an important part, must certainly be taken into account by every student of Victorian taste in the arts; and when we consider, in addition, the impact made by the Pre-Raphaelites from 1848 onwards, it is not difficult to guess, at least, at the nature of the distractions (if we may call them that) which would have drawn public attention away from the older tradition of English landscape painting in which the art of Boys had its origins, and to which it properly belongs. Nor, I imagine, would the gentle reserve of Boys's style have easily withstood the more spectacular effects of such popular, but more superficial, painters as David Cox, J.D. Harding, James Holland and William Callow, whose free handling and dashing colouring may well have appeared to the Victorians as not only more imaginative than Boys's subtler qualities, but as more 'artistic'.

If this was so, Boys would have suffered much as De Wint did from that Victorian taste for often gaudy colour which was encouraged by the ideals of the Pre-Raphaelites, whose innovations in the use of dazzlingly brilliant colour-orchestrations placed them in a superior category of their own. Two incidents recorded by Callow in his autobiography may be significant in this context. After working in Paris in close association with Boys, whose manner he imitated, Callow returned to London in his thirtieth year and at once became famous for the watercolours which he exhibited at the Old Water-colour Society. While appealing to the new taste, he had absorbed much of Boys's skill in harmonizing his compositions, and in fact his early work appealed to Thackeray on account of its very moderation. Thackeray's reviews of art exhibitions, published in *Fraser's Magazine* under the pseudonym of Michael Angelo Titmarsh, were much respected at the time, and his praise of Callow must have helped to establish the young artist's reputation, just as Ruskin's neglect of Boys must have worked to the older artist's disadvantage. Callow's arrival in England from Paris had been heralded by the following commendation in one of Thackeray's reviews:

> A new painter, somewhat in the style of Harding, is Mr Callow; and better, I think, than his master or original, whose colours are too gaudy, to my taste, and effects too glaringly theatrical.

As Callow himself observed, 'Success seemed, therefore, assured.' It was indeed, and Callow had the good fortune to attract the attention of the Royal family and various aristocratic patrons.

At the exhibition of 1852, which was visited by Queen Victoria and Prince Albert, the Queen and the Prince Consort made a point of conversing with Callow, and both bought drawings by him on that occasion. The New Water-colour Society, of which Boys was a member, seems not to have enjoyed the reputation or popularity of the Old Water-colour Society.

The second incident to which I have alluded again concerns an exhibition at the Old Water-colour Society, and it is best told in Callow's own words:

> At one of the Exhibitions a bright drawing of mine, full of Italian sunshine, was placed on the line next to another by Peter De Wint, which, although very powerful in colour, was dark in tone. He considered that mine placed his at a disadvantage, and suggested to me that I should subdue my drawing by placing a warm tint all over it. Needless to say my brother artists advised me to take no notice of the suggestion, which, if it had been carried out, would have ruined my work.

The relative quietude of De Wint's style has much in common with that of Boys; and Boys, although a younger man than De Wint by some seventeen years, owed much to the older tradition as developed by Girtin, whose influence on both De Wint and Boys was clearly very considerable. A watercolour by either Girtin or Boys, hung next to a typical work by Callow, would have been likely to suffer quite unjustly from the juxtaposition. Moreover, if we turn back to the pages of Ruskin, we shall discover that, while he often refers to De Wint, he seems to have found him lacking in imagination and too devoted to the truth of appearances, a criticism which he might have put forward with reference to Boys. As he wrote in the first volume of *Modern Painters*:

> There is too much that is instructive and deserving of high praise in the sketches of De Wint. Yet it is to be remembered that even the pursuit of truth, however determined, will have results limited and imperfect when its chief motive is the pride of being true; and I fear that these works testify more accuracy of eye and experience of colour than exercise of thought.

The contrast between faint praise of this kind and Ruskin's treatment of such artists as Copley Fielding, Clarkson Stanfield, David Roberts and, not least, Samuel Prout is a striking one.

There can be no doubt that, soon after the successful publication of *London as it is,* Boys sank gradually into neglect. In the previous year, a critic writing in *The Art Union* (later to be renamed *The Art Journal*) had remarked, 'No painter approaches Mr Boys.' It may, however, be the case that the publication of *London as it is* obscured Boys's merits as a watercolourist, as distinct from a lithographer. The earlier series of *Picturesque Architecture* had been based upon superb watercolours, which remain Boys's masterpieces in the medium. On the other hand, as James Roundell shows, the *Views of London as it is* were executed without the intermediary of watercolour drawings. If such watercolours had existed, and had been available for exhibition, it is difficult to think that they would not have helped considerably to keep Boys's work as a watercolourist in the forefront of public and critical attention.

The position of Thomas Shotter Boys in the history of the English watercolour school has never been fully examined, and has been obscured by the emphasis which has been placed upon the tradition that Boys was Bonington's pupil. James Roundell's researches have revealed valuable new information which helps to establish the exact nature of their relationship. Bonington's influence on Boys was clearly profound and long-lasting. However, while Boys was in Paris he was conscious of his role as Girtin's successor in the depiction of Paris scenes, and at the same time he was full of admiration for Girtin's work. This historical connection between Boys and Girtin is exceptionally interesting: and the further link between Girtin and Francia, of which we also have documentation, is important in the context of Girtin's influence upon the Bonington circle in Paris, of which Boys was a leading member. It has long been recognized that Girtin was a revolutionary figure in the history of English watercolour, and that it was he, more than Turner or any other contemporary, who was responsible for the liberation of watercolour from its earlier limitations, so that by the early nineteenth century its full potentialities could be realized and even accepted as worthy of comparison with those of oil-painting. It was to the innovations introduced by Girtin (who died young in 1802) that Boys and his contemporaries fell heir; and there is much in Boys's art that suggests his admiration of Girtin as a watercolourist.

The older tradition is summed up in the work of Paul Sandby, who was probably born (according to the findings of recent research) in 1731. Although Sandby's range was wider than is often thought, and although he made experiments in the use of body-colour, the basis of his method remained the accepted technique of the *tinted drawing*. Today we think of watercolour as a branch of painting; but at the time when Sandby's style was formed such a concept would have been unthinkable: in eighteenth-century England watercolour was considered a branch of drawing, and the word *painting* always designated painting in oils. In consequence, watercolourists who exhibited at the Royal Academy found their work hung together with architectural drawings or in rooms reserved for sculpture: since a watercolour was not considered to be a painting, the artists had a genuine grievance when they began to complain that their work was not given the prominence accorded to pictures in oils. This conflict was to see the establishment, in the first part of the nineteenth century, of the various watercolour societies which enabled artists painting in watercolour to exhibit their work separately. As Hardie relates, these societies attempted to compete with the Royal Academy by showing large, elaborate watercolours rivalling oil-paintings in size and finish. Gradually the Royal Academy accepted the new status of the art of watercolour painting. In fact in 1841, when Boys was elected a member of the New Water-colour Society, Roberts enjoyed the greater honour of being made a Royal Academician. Although Boys was to exhibit at the Academy in 1847 and 1848, whatever hopes he may have entertained of emulating Roberts's success were not fulfilled; and thereafter, until shortly before his death in 1874, he continued to show his watercolours at the New Water-colour Society.

The foundation of these watercolour societies and the eventual change in the Academy's attitude towards watercolour painting were developments of fundamental importance in which the innovatory art of Thomas Girtin has a central place. Girtin himself had been trained, under Edward Dayes, in the old tradition of the tinted drawing; and in his early work, like his friend Turner in the same period, he still made use of the grey washes which were characteristic of the old technique and which had the function of establishing the tones of all the forms before the final tints were applied. His contemporary W. H. Pyne, himself both painter and critic, has left us a long account, written in 1824, of Girtin's technique in his later watercolours, in which this procedure was abandoned in favour of an immediate application of local colour without the preliminary underpainting. Pyne drew a comparison between Girtin's method and that of the oil-painters, and although it would be mistaken to suppose that painters in oil had all abandoned the use of an underpainting, it is clear enough that Girtin and, of course, Turner did aim at effects that would rival those obtainable in oil-painting—achieving a greater strength and richness of colour. Indeed, it later became the normal custom to exhibit watercolours in heavy gilt frames, in order to demonstrate that watercolours could compete with oil-paintings on their own ground. As Pyne observed of an exhibition of the Painters in Water-Colours, '. . . pictures of this class were displayed in gorgeous frames, bearing out in effect against the mass of glittering gold, as powerfully as pictures in oil.'

Although Girtin had been anticipated in this departure from tradition by Francis Towne and others, and although he himself often employed a warm preparatory wash, or underpainting, it was he who developed the new method within the terms, as it were, of a correspondingly new vision, which opened up vistas hitherto unglimpsed. In his hands the art of watercolour came to maturity: on a technical level, his achievement is comparable with that of Titian in the art of oil-painting; for, as in late Titian drawing, tone and colour cease to have separate functions, but are blended into a total, unified process, so it is with Girtin in the watercolours executed shortly before his death. Yet, by comparison with many of his successors in the nineteenth century, the most outstanding difference that strikes the eye is the new sense of *tonal* harmony. That is not to undervalue the novel richness and depth of Girtin's colour; but whereas many of his followers carried his innovations in colouring to the point of exaggeration and excess, few of them understood, or were gifted enough to emulate, the superb resonance of his tonalities.

One artist who, I feel sure, did appreciate this quality in Girtin's late watercolours was Thomas Shotter Boys. Another was De Wint; and perhaps when De Wint tried to insist that Callow should tone down the dashingly coloured work which had been so uncongenially hung on the line next to one of his own watercolours, he was aware especially of the difference between his own quiet concern for tonal melodies and the meretricious brilliance of Callow's colouring. We have definite evidence of Girtin's lasting influence upon De Wint; and I believe that the stylistic evidence points to a similar link between Girtin and Boys.

At the same time it was from Bonington that Boys derived a type of spacious composition in which the grandeur of a building or the charm of a vista is emphasized by an attention to *scale*; and it was likewise Bonington, as well as Prout, who showed him the value of introducing a variety of figures glimpsed in the act of going about their daily business, and thus lending both vividness and an air of informality to a particular view. But the first of these characteristics of Boys's art had already been anticipated by Girtin, as, for example, in his *Porte St Denis* (in the Victoria and Albert Museum, London), where the space given to the sky and the scale of the architecture in relation to an emphatically spacious design may remind us more of Boys than of Bonington.

Again, where Bonington was often careless in his treatment of perspective, Boys, like Girtin before him, was punctilious in his attention to it; and the complex perspectival structure of Girtin's *Porte St Denis* can be matched by numerous examples from Boys's designs for the *Picturesque Architecture*. Perhaps the truth of the matter is that in Bonington perspective often serves an essentially dramatic purpose, so that a particular building seen at an oblique angle does not merely recede, but thrusts into space. Like Girtin, Boys eschews such dramatic effects, and, to take a representative example, his *Quai de la Grève* of 1837 (Plate 48) illustrates the point to perfection: the mood is one of quietude, as in Girtin, and the exquisitely arranged colours are eloquent, not of a powerfully dramatic vision, but of an ideal of delicate serenity. So it is also with Boys's lighting, which is equally undramatic (whereas in Bonington it is often forced up to a pitch of expressive conflict between light and dark), and flows evenly through his compositions, with the consequence that lights and darks blend together in a total, almost liquid harmony; and here too we are reminded of the tonal mastery of Girtin. Moreover the clarity and habitual lack of incident in Boys's placid skies are no less characteristic of a style which, although owing much to Bonington's example, preserves its own distinctiveness.

Its quietude, which I have stressed earlier, is summed up in his treatment of the figures that often people his compositions in great numbers. In this he differs greatly from Girtin, who evidently lacked the interest in contemporary life and in its modes and manners which both Prout and Boys observed with a curious and sometimes humorous eye. Ruskin, we recall, wrote of Prout that 'his markets are the only markets where one feels inclined to get out of the way',

16

and that, in the case of other topographical artists, 'we feel the figures so right where they are . . . and approve of the position of the man with the wheelbarrow, without the slightest fear of his running it against our legs'. There is, as it happens, a man with a wheelbarrow in the *Quai de la Grève,* of which Ruskin could have been thinking. Although it is being pushed in our direction, and although it serves the function of adding incident to the whole left side of the foreground, it is placed at a decent distance, and the man turns his head aside to look back into the scene, where a street orator is addressing a small crowd; like every other figure present, he takes up his appointed position in the composition; and, as Ruskin's words invite us to do, we cannot but approve: the whole design is so skilful, and so perfectly realized, that it would be difficult to find a composition by any contemporary to surpass it in its delicately balanced harmony.

We return therefore to that fundamental 'classicism' which distinguished Boys from both Prout and Bonington, that concern with pure relationships of shape and colour which we are accustomed to admire especially in the art of Cotman. Whether or not there was any connection between the styles of Cotman and Boys (as indeed may be doubted), some of the values that raise Cotman far above the level of most of his contemporaries are certainly found again in Boys, but in the context of very different subject-matter. If Boys's range was limited, and if he lacked the imagination of a Bonington or the poetry of a Girtin, he shared with Cotman a sense of the primacy of design; and perhaps the passage which I have quoted from Ruskin conceals a grudging admiration of this fundamental concern with the subtleties of pictorial composition.

Besides the qualities that I have touched upon, Boys stands in the vanguard of that development in English and French painting of the early nineteenth century towards *pleinairisme*. Like Girtin and Constable before him, and like Bonington, he recognized the value of the sky in an open-air scene, whether it was a townscape or a landscape; and the luminosity of his usually calm skies sets the key for his compositions, which he bathes in a cool, pervasive light observed (as it can only have been) directly from the *motif*. Indeed few of his contemporaries approach him in his ability to suggest the radiance of noonday light or the glow of sunny afternoons. And it is in the context of this feeling for light and its properties that we must see him in relation to Girtin; for the mastery of tonal values which, as I have suggested, he may well have learnt, at least in part, from Girtin cannot be separated from his evident desire to achieve luminosity in his watercolours, as also in his lithographs. This feeling was wholly modern in its intention. His tonal harmonies, accordingly, are often pitched higher than those of Girtin, and the resulting melody is lighter. The beauty of the individual plates in *London as it is,* in which, in the coloured versions, he translated his watercolour practice directly into the terms of lithography, resides in great measure in the luminous clarity of the lighting itself.

I end with this marvellous work, just as I began with it, because of its great importance both in the history of lithography and in the history of English topographical art. It belongs, of course, to its own age, and must be judged in that context: but it may be said in conclusion that what Thomas Rowlandson did for the Regency period, whether in his glimpses of London life or, more generally, in his *Tour of Dr Syntax in Search of the Picturesque* (of 1812), Thomas Shotter Boys did for the early Victorians. Besides Rowlandson, Boys is sedate, and his humour is quaint rather than boisterous; Boys usually observes the proprieties, whereas Rowlandson delights in the improprieties, so that we almost remember him by them. In brief, the comparison leaves us with the impression that Rowlandson shows us London as it had been, while Boys depicts London as it should be. But Boys's achievement was such that we shall always see the London of the first years of Queen Victoria's reign through his eyes.

I
EARLY LIFE

COMING from an old and distinguished English family, Thomas Shotter Boys was born on 2 January 1803. His grandfather had lived in Lincolnshire before moving to Hendon, near London. His son, James Boys, the artist's father, lived for most of his life in White Lion Street, Pentonville, where Thomas Shotter Boys was born. James Boys, in contrast to other members of the family, was never well off.[1] By profession a salesman (though of what it is not known) James Boys married Elizabeth Collins, who originally came from Bath. They only had two children, Thomas Shotter and his younger sister, Mary. Elizabeth survived James who left her all his money and property except the proceeds of the sale of the house in White Lion Street, which were to be distributed equally between herself, Thomas Shotter and Mary.[2]

Very little is known of Shotter Boys's early life and education before his father's death. However, he must have shown some early skill at drawing as he was apprenticed, on 4 February 1817, to George Cooke.[3] Cooke, one of the best-known and most successful engravers of his day, ran a flourishing studio in Barnes. Among the works engraved by Cooke and his studio during Boys's apprenticeship were Turner's *Picturesque Views on the Southern Coast of England* (1814–26); Allason's *Antiquities of Pola* (1819); Hakewill's *Picturesque Tour of Italy* (1820) and George Cooke's own production *The Thames* (1822). So Boys was lucky enough to see and study closely works of the leading artists of the day, which must have stirred his ambitions.

The first known dated work by Boys is a drawing of a *Scorpion* (Plate 1), signed and dated 1819. The *Lizard* (Plate 2), though undated, must be from the same period. These are small, unambitious studies which a young apprentice might well have had to execute as part of his training. One of his fellow students was Edward William Cooke, George's son, and although Edward was eight years younger than Boys they soon struck up a firm friendship.[4] A letter, written by Edward to his father in 1820, tells of an amusing diversion:

> If I write a very good copy and do another sum, may I model toms ear in wax for thomas boys. He has given me wax and tools and with the other part of the wax I can model something for you. I Remain Your Affectionate, dutiful and Benevolent son E. W. Cooke.[5]

Presumably Boys, while still a pupil, worked on certain publications for which George Cooke prepared the engravings, but being a mere student he was not credited with the work. George Cooke was engaged to engrave all the plates for Loddiges' *Botanical Cabinet* (1818–33) but it is known that Boys made drawings for 194 of the plates, all of which were inscribed with his name (Plates 3 and 4). The first of the latter was No. 811 in Volume Nine, published in 1824. By that time Boys was no longer a pupil but an independent artist, and as such was credited with the work. It is more than likely that he was making drawings for this series even while he was an apprentice.

There are no other works known to be by Boys before the termination of his apprenticeship in 1823. Ottley's statement that Boys 'drew some thousand illustrations on wood for Loudon's *Cyclopaedia of Plants*' seems to be ungrounded;[6] there is no mention of his name in that book.

The 1819 drawings show that Boys must have been taught to draw correctly, and to master

18

the intricacies of volume and perspective. However, due to the fact that Cooke was primarily an etcher and engraver, more emphasis in Boys's training must have been placed on these skills rather than on painting. He undoubtedly would have learnt how to use the graving burin to draw a firm line and build up a consistent area of shade, and also he would have been taught the correct manner in which to lay down aquatint washes and to hand-colour prints. His qualifications were those of an engraver; he had not received an academic art training.

It has been assumed, following Ottley's guide, that Boys left for Paris in 1825, but there is evidence to the contrary. His apprenticeship was for a term of seven years ending on 4 February 1824; however, it is likely that Boys left Cooke's studio earlier as there is an etching by him of an *Ancient Vase*, taken from the collection of Baron Denon, dated 1823 and published in Paris.[7] Furthermore, in Volume Three of *Blackie's History of England* there is a view of *Le Prison de l'Abbaye, Paris*, inscribed: *Drawn by T. Boys, from his sketch made on the spot, 1824*.[8] In the same year he exhibited a picture of a *Vase* at the galleries of the Society of British Artists in Suffolk Street; in the list of exhibitors' addresses his was left blank, which perhaps adds strength to the theory that he was in France at the time. Ottley claimed that Boys exhibited at the Royal Academy in 1822 and 1823—an extravagant but false claim for a nineteen-year-old pupil who still had two years of his apprenticeship to fulfil. The only explanation for these inconsistencies is that Boys had left Cooke's studio in either 1822 or 1823 before his apprenticeship was formally finished.

His father had died in 1821, leaving instructions to sell the family house in White Lion Street; and Boys's share of the proceeds, on the assumption that the house was sold, would have provided him with the means to go to France. He went to Paris as an engraver, not a painter. Ottley states that he was 'employed on engraving by Denon, Mazois, Gau, Hillorff *(sic)* and Zanth, and Baron Humboldt'. These were auspicious patrons for a young and unknown English engraver in Paris—a reflection on the dearth of engravers resident in Paris during the 1820s. In those days twenty was not considered too young for an artist to start a career in a foreign country. In 1829, for example, at the age of only seventeen, William Callow left the service of Theodore Fielding in London to go to Paris and assist a Mr Ostervald in aquatint engraving. The romantic attraction of the Continent—and particularly of Paris, which had been the focus of the French Revolution—was undoubtedly part of this desire to leave England.

Boys did not completely sever his connections with England after he had left, for he must have made return visits to carry out work on the *Botanical Cabinet* for George Cooke, his old master. He may also have returned in November 1823 for the marriage of his sister Mary to William John Cooke, E. W. Cooke's cousin, which further strengthened his lifelong friendship with the Cooke family.

NOTES TO CHAPTER ONE

1 See Appendix A.
2 Somerset House. Will dated 16 August 1805.
3 The original indenture of apprenticeship is in the possession of C. R. Cooke, O.B.E.
4 The only portrait of Shotter Boys (*see* title page) shows him in the company of E. W. Cooke.
5 In the collection of C. R. Cooke, O.B.E. E. W. Cooke's precocity is well attested. *The Art Journal* of 1869 (page 253), possibly exaggerating, says that 'Before he had reached his ninth year he was engaged in drawing upon wood several thousand plants from nature, in the nursery grounds of Messrs Loddiges, Hackney, to illustrate *Loudon's Encyclopaedia of Plants*.'
6 It is possible that in his *Biographical and critical dictionary of recent and living painters and engravers*, London, 1866, Ottley got his information from Boys himself as the entry was written in the latter's lifetime.
7 Bibliothèque Nationale, Paris.
8 Volume Three, page 850.

II
PARIS

I T is a strange coincidence that a branch of the Boys family came from a village in Kent called
Bonington,[1] for the next period of Boys's artistic activity is dominated, rightly or wrongly,
by the name Bonington. Richard Parkes Bonington was one of the most famous practitioners
of watercolour painting. Born in Nottingham in 1802, he moved to France in 1817 with his
parents. There he was taught watercolour painting in the style of Thomas Girtin by Louis
Francia. Bonington became the main initiator of the romantic fluid manner of painting in both
oils and watercolours (Figures I and II).

He did not enjoy fame in England during his lifetime, and even in France he was regarded as
an immature member of the brilliant new generation of artists which included such as Delacroix
and Géricault. His rise to fame was one of those strange quirks of fashion which seem to overtake
society from time to time. The romantic image of the youthful English artist who fled to Paris,
where he died a premature and tragic death, caught the imagination of society and the acquisitive
instincts of the dealers. In 1834 the *Morning Chronicle* declared:

> He died, and fashion made him an idol; and simpleheaded collectors have humoured folly-fashion
> to the top of her bent . . . We could have excused the extravagance had it spent itself on Bonington
> himself, but his empty shadow has come in for a vast share. Copies and imitations have been multi-
> plied and spread in all directions.[2]

In the previous year *The Magazine of Fine Arts* stated:

> The cupidity of dealers has been so great that caution and perception are now necessary in buying a
> Bonington. As in the case of Girtin, imitation is daily at work to ensnare the collector.[3]

It is rare for an artist to receive the approbation of his contemporaries to the extent which
Bonington did, although he did not live to enjoy it. However, this blind adoration had wider
implications; one of them was to overshadow the rising star of Thomas Shotter Boys—a shadow
from which he never escaped.

It is difficult to extract the truth from the legend of Richard Parkes Bonington. What was the
exact nature of the relationship between Bonington and Boys, both in their art and in their lives?
It is widely assumed that Bonington was many years the senior of Boys in age, but in fact he
was only just over two months older. He had gone to France at the age of fifteen, and in 1820
he entered the Ecole des Beaux Arts in the atelier of Baron Gros. There his fellow students
included Huet, Delacroix and Roqueplan. He left the Gros atelier in the winter of 1822. So he
was beginning his career as an independent artist at about the same time as Boys arrived in Paris.

The Magazine of Fine Arts of 1833 states that 'J. Bays *(sic)*, a watercolour painter, was a pupil
of Bonington.'[4] Callow, in his autobiography, says:

> In later years I have seen it stated that Boys was a pupil of Bonington, but if that had been the case
> I certainly should have known of it. Boys never spoke to me of having other than a mere acquain-
> tanceship with Bonington.[5]

Here lies the basis of the confusion surrounding the issue of whether Boys was a pupil of Bonington. The English journalist maintains that he was, but manages to write his name and initial

wrongly. Callow, writing seventy years later, suggests the reverse.[6] Most recent writers have followed Ottley's remark that Boys was persuaded by Bonington 'to leave engraving and take to painting', and have said that Boys was his pupil.

Though probably to some extent correct, this does not reveal the whole story. There were not many English artists working in Paris in 1823. It is more than likely that Bonington would have welcomed Boys as a new companion, and would have treated him as an equal rather than as an inferior. The relationship prior to 1825 is still obscure, but in that year Bonington made a trip to England in the company of Delacroix and Isabey. There he met W. J. Cooke who, one year later, engraved Bonington's *Rouen from Bon Secours*. This introduction must surely have been made by Boys, and offers proof of their early friendship.

From May 1826 Bonington took a studio at 11 Rue des Martyrs in Paris, where he remained until February 1828. During this time several contacts with Boys are recorded which help to illuminate the exact nature of their relationship. In May of 1826 Bonington had visited Italy with Baron Rivet, and it is for dinner with Rivet and a few friends that he invites Boys to his atelier at Rue des Martyrs:

> Dear Boys,
>   Try and come this evening Rivet and a few friends will be here, avec the french model & tout cela pour rejouir le chretien M. Auguste à qui appartiennent les honneurs de la soires ne sera pas moins aise de vous voir que
>
>   votre ami
>   Bonington
>   ce Mardi Matin[7]

This was addressed to Boys at 15 Rue de la Rochefoucauld, where he must have had a lodging or an atelier at the time. Rue de la Rochefoucauld is in fact only three streets away from Rue des Martyrs; Boys was virtually Bonington's neighbour. The letter conveys a tone of close friendship, and the easy switch from one language to another conveys the informal nature of their relationship.

The British Museum possesses a drawing of the interior of Bonington's atelier, drawn by Boys. It shows various pictures of Venice propped up against the walls and on the easel, and must have been done after Bonington's return from Italy while he was still working on Venetian themes. Boys must have been a constant visitor to his friend's studio, and no doubt dashed this drawing off on one such visit. A watercolour of *Les Salinières by Trouville* (Plate 5) by Bonington bears the inscription on the verso, reputedly in Boys's hand: 'Drawn for me by R.P. Bonington to show me the place of Chancre, 1826. Rue des Martyrs. Thos. S. Boys.' This further underlines their close and unselfish friendship.

In 1828 Bonington became very ill with tuberculosis and it is probable that his last few months in Paris were inactive ones, spent mostly in a chair or on his sickbed. Finally it became necessary for him to return to England to obtain a cure (alas, unsuccessful) at the hands of St John Long, a fashionable crank doctor. Boys may well have accompanied him back to England. John Saddler, the engraver, in a letter written to Messrs Shepherd Bros, said:

> I was a pupil of William John Cooke, the engraver, and close friend of Bonington, and had been a month with him when Bonington came to dinner. I have some curious reminiscences of the day. It happened that my master was, at the instigation of his brother-in-law, Thomas Shotter Boys, making experiments for a permanent brown ink over which colour could be washed. One of the materials was walnut juice extracted from the outside shells and boiled down to expel the watery particles—and Bonington after dinner, while reclining on two or three chairs, made sundry sketches, with pencil and brush with the juice, and expressed his intention when he was better he should try the material further, adding his approbation of the colour—permanency had not been tried. They were brought into the study to be thrown into the paper basket, but I took care of them, with Mr

Cooke's permission, and I have them now, and have sent them herewith, also a pencil sketch by Bonington given me by Mr Boys . . . They are simply curious (the ink sketches) as the very last things Bonington produced—he died after that visit.[8]

Thus Boys was with Bonington shortly before his death. The depth of affection which this suggests Boys felt is perhaps best expressed in his own words:

When I called . . . I had brought down a drawing or 2 of Bonington's to shew you I say shew you as I really cannot find it in my heart to part with one of them.[9]

Shotter Boys's artistic debt to Bonington presents many problems for the investigator. Bonington is thought to have painted about thirteen hundred works—oils, watercolours, drawings and prints—during his lifetime. At the time of Bonington's death Boys had produced fewer than ten that are documented. It is not surprising, then, that Martin Hardie should remark that 'it seems impossible to account for the comparative rarity of watercolours by Boys except by assuming that very many . . . have been absorbed and submerged in Bonington's *oeuvre*.'[10]

It has been difficult to appraise the true qualities of Bonington's work because of his legendary aura, and it is certainly not the intention here to give a detailed analysis of his style.[11] In a study devoted to Shotter Boys, it is essential to consider in what respects his style approaches to, and differs from, that of Bonington. The latter was taught by Francia—a disciple of Girtin—and subsequently by Baron Gros. Bonington studied with Delacroix and their respective early styles are extremely similar. From Francia he learnt the method of laying down a smooth and translucent wash of watercolour in the English manner. From Baron Gros and Delacroix he learnt the richness of colour and feeling characteristic of the French school of painting. In France he was taught according to the academic norm: he drew figure subjects, copied old masters and practised oil painting. It is no surprise that he was to paint a high proportion of figurative and historical pictures.

Boys had had an entirely different training. He had learnt the engraver's trade without any of the academic trimmings of the Ecole des Beaux Arts. He was taught neither oil painting nor figure drawing in the classical mode. As an engraver he chiefly mastered the skills of line, tone and wash. His scope was never as wide as Bonington's; he painted few figurative or historical subjects, and relatively few oil paintings. His main subject matter was landscape and townscape.

It is likely that Boys was employed as an engraver immediately on his arrival in Paris; like Callow, he may even have been recruited in England for work in France. It may have been one or two years before he was free to turn his attention towards watercolour painting and be instructed by his friend Bonington—as inferred by Ottley. The absence of attributed or attributable watercolours for the years 1824–26 supports this theory.

To gain an idea of his style during the period prior to Bonington's death, there is only a handful of dated works which can be studied. The sepia pen drawing of Bonington's studio suggests nothing that a competent engraver could not have done, except for a mastery of the enclosed spatial perspective of the studio. His watercolour of *Les Salinières* (Plate 6) is more rewarding, and is certainly not the work of a beginner. It shows confidence in the use of colour, the application of watercolour and in the creation of mood. He uses techniques such as scratching out whites with a knife and employs the stub end of the brush on the water. It is just a slight sketch, but in its freedom and handling it conveys a certain maturity. All the technical characteristics and the general colour range of the work are found in Bonington's watercolours of this period. However, the conception of the scene is different from that of Bonington (Plate 5) who treats it more romantically in terms of composition and more lightly in his brushwork. Boys's washes

I   II

FIGURE I **THE LEANING TOWER, BOLOGNA,** by Richard Parkes Bonington (1803–28).
Watercolour, $9\frac{1}{4} \times 6\frac{3}{4}$ ins/235 × 172 mm.
The Wallace Collection, London.
Reproduced by Permission of the Trustees of the Wallace Collection.

FIGURE II **L'INSTITUT DE FRANCE,** by Richard Parkes Bonington (1803–28).
Watercolour, $9\frac{5}{8} \times 7\frac{15}{16}$ ins/245 × 202 mm.
British Museum, London (1919.2.12.224).
Photograph by courtesy of the Trustees of the British Museum.

Overleaf
FIGURE III **PARIS FROM BERCY,** by William Callow (1812–1908).
Pencil, $4\frac{3}{16} \times 11\frac{1}{8}$ ins/106 × 283 mm.
Inscribed (BR) Saturday July 6th 1831 from Bercy
Victoria and Albert Museum, London (E.877–1937).
Reproduced by courtesy of the Victoria and Albert Museum.

FIGURE IV **HOTEL DE SENS, PARIS,** by William Callow (1812–1908).
Pencil, $7\frac{9}{16} \times 9\frac{1}{4}$ ins/192 × 235 mm.
Inscribed (BL) Juin 29th 1832
Victoria and Albert Museum, London (E.894–1937).
Reproduced by courtesy of the Victoria and Albert Museum.

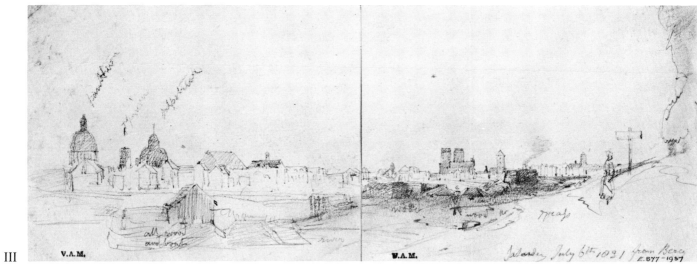

III   V.A.M.   V.A.M.   E.877-1937

IV   V.A.M.   E.894-1937

24

are uniformly dryer and more harmonious, but he may have lacked adventure in the use of brilliant colour and the confidence of Bonington's fluent brushwork. The *Tour d'Alexandre et la Fontaine Saint Victor* (1827)[12] shows a different facet of his early style. It is a free sketch of a slight subject treated with bold wet washes which the artist was not quite able to control. The conclusion is that Boys was not yet a master of his craft.

By 1829 and 1830 his talents revealed themselves in such works as *Le Pavillon de Flore*,[13] *L'Institut de France*[14] (Plate 15) and *Hôtel de Bellevue and the Café d'Amitié seen from the Park, Brussels* (Plate 14). In these watercolours most of the techniques employed by Bonington are found—dragged washes of dry colour, paper highlights scratched out with the aid of a knife or the stub end of the brush, paper left showing between different washes to form part of the colour composition, gum to add depth to the darkest tones, the superimposition of washes without their mixing and touches of bodycolour to give accents to the general colour range. However, there is an essential difference in the conception of the subject: Boys concentrates more on what is in front of him, drawing the solid lines and forms of the scene rather than its evanescent and impermanent features. Bonington's buildings (Figures I and II) do not have the solidity and precision of Boys's architecture, they are picturesque elements of the composition, not the *raison d'être* of the painting. He concentrates his attention on the portrayal of the atmosphere of the scene at a precise moment; the forms of the figures have been stopped for an instant in their passage across the picture, the scudding clouds he has captured in a few quick and fluid washes of blue. His style is one of instinct; he paints what his highly sensitive emotions register.

This is not to say that Boys did not have a feeling for a scene. He simply responded in a different way, being filled with love and admiration for what he saw rather than with more spontaneous artistic urges; and what he saw is vividly expressed in the words of William Callow:

> Boys used frequently to ramble about the ancient part of the Cité of Paris in search of old buildings to sketch . . . and it was from him I first acquired my love for making watercolour drawings of picturesque old churches and houses . . . The streets, which were lighted by oil lanterns suspended down the middle by cords, were laid with cobblestones with gutters running down the centre, and without any side pavements.[15]

This is what Boys always loved to portray in his pictures. Although he painted several figurative and historical paintings, *e.g.* Plate 19, it was the appearance and activity of the town that attracted him. He executed many sea- and landscapes, but they provoke the feeling that, though immersed in his subject, he did not respond with the sensibility and the romantic faculties of Bonington when confronted by such scenes. Boys used the latter's techniques to paint the same views, the artistic contrast arising from the different characters of the two artists.

What sort of person was Boys? Again there is a lack of biographical information; his contemporaries recorded for posterity only a few remarks. Only two portraits of him exist, one by his own hand—and that almost a caricature. It appears in the foreground of *The Tower and Mint, from Great Tower Hill* in *London as it is* (*see* jacket). It shows the artist sketching the scene surrounded by a group of children. To them he must have been a curious sight, this rather rotund gentleman dressed in tails and a tall hat (hardly the clothes for an afternoon's sketching). It is scenes such as this which delighted Boys; he loved to include amusing and characteristic pieces of genre in his pictures. In other works he depicts men sleeping in doorways, constructing scaffolding, pulling up the road, watching balloons, and even relieving themselves against walls. This all suggests a keen perception of life and a strong sense of humour. The fine architectural detail in his lithographs and watercolours testify to his powers of observation, and the fact that the only other known portrait of him was painted while he was playing cards provides evidence of his sense of humour (*see* title page).

Boys's own letters add certain elements to this picture. When roused, he was not averse to using strong language: 'Damn the Belgians God damn and blast the bloody Belgians.'[16]

On another occasion, when mocking the use artists made of sketching stools, he expressed himself with similar forthrightness: '. . . . an artist brings his a--e to the ground or stands'.[17] He continued in a cynical tone: 'So now you are about to be the rich man don't refuse me the crumbs that may fall from your table.'

Despite these remarks, there is a warmth of tone in his early letters which suggests an easy and friendly character. There is something of the gentleman in the outrage he expressed at other people's practices when he complains that certain publications 'are the damndest, lying, ill got up, money getting clap-trap possible' and he was 'soured by publishers' and that 'Mitchell has swindled all the world here'.[18] He exhibits here a feeling for what is proper and correct; in his work, too, these same qualities form the basis of his watercolour style.

His friendship with E. W. Cooke was evidently very strong until about 1840, for until that date Boys's name featured often in Cooke's diaries.[19] Unfortunately, in these notebooks there are no remarks about Boys's character. Nor did Callow record much in this respect in his rather belated autobiography (tantalisingly uninformative about these early years), in which he refers to Boys as 'the clever but eccentric artist'.[20] Edward Webb (1805–54) tells of 'a young man named Boys, very clever'.[21] 'Eccentric' is a difficult word to interpret at the best of times, but it would probably be wrong to infer that it was used here as a reflection on Boys's mental stability.

The years immediately after Bonington's death were apparently busy ones for Boys. He complains in a letter of 1831 that he must write a brief note only as 'from want of time it must be short'[22] and, later on in the same letter, that he could not execute some drawings because he 'was engaged to get up a certain commission within a given time'. He must have thrived on this work since he adds a little footnote: 'P.S. Never so well!' The forewarnings of later disasters that were to overtake him are shown when he complains that he suffers 'considerably of the general shortness of cash'.[23]

From these words it appears that he was heavily engaged by French printers and publishers to do bread-and-butter engravings for their publications, work which does not seem to have been financially rewarding. These years also saw an expansion of his watercolour practice. This increased demand on his time and resources may have been the reason he decided to share a studio in Rue du Bouloy with Callow.[24] In Callow he no doubt saw a young Englishman with much the same qualifications and style as himself (Figures IV, V and XIII), who might be able to help out if he was overworked. In his autobiography Callow relates how he made some sketches from the bridges of Paris for Boys (Plate 25); how when he was in England he made sketches in Pall Mall and Richmond for him, and how he delivered a present from Boys to George Cooke, and a Turkish sword to John Constable.[25]

Ambrose Poynter was another artist with whom Boys was closely associated in these early years. Although older than Boys, it seems that he came to Paris in 1832 and was for a short time his pupil.[26] He was an architect and readily appreciated the careful draughtsmanship with which Boys drew his buildings. Boys taught Poynter to paint in watercolour and there are many drawings from around this time which show how much he owed stylistically to Boys (Figure VII).

In these early years Boys often repeated the subjects that he painted in what sometimes appear

26

V

VI

Arc de Triomphe de l'Et. Paris. 7. 9 août 1830

VII   VIII

Previous page
FIGURE V **L'ESCALIER DE L'ORANGERIE A VERSAILLES,** by William Callow (1812–1908).
Watercolour, $5 \times 7\frac{13}{16}$ ins/127 × 199 mm.
Inscribed (BL) <u>A Versailles Aout 18 1832</u>
          (Verso) <u>26/Versailles William Callow</u>
Fondation Custodia, Institut Néerlandais, Paris (1972.T.67).

FIGURE VI **CONSTRUCTION OF THE ARC DE TRIOMPHE,** by Joseph Nash (1808–78).
Pencil, $8\frac{7}{8} \times 11\frac{7}{16}$ ins/225 × 290 mm.
Signed (B) <u>Arc de Triomphe de l'Etoile J. Nash 1830</u>
          (TL) <u>No. 24</u>
          (Verso) : <u>size for the/wood Engraving/for Mr Knight</u>
Fondation Custodia, Institut Néerlandais, Paris (1971.T.56).

This page
FIGURE VII **RUE ST ROMAN, ROUEN,** by Ambrose Poynter (1796–1886).
Watercolour, $10 \times 6\frac{5}{8}$ ins/254 × 168 mm.
Signed (BL) <u>A Poynter/1837</u>
British Museum, London (1942.10.10.7).
Photograph by courtesy of the Trustees of the British Museum.

FIGURE VIII **THE ABBEY OF ST ARMAND,** by Richard Parkes Bonington (1803–28).
Watercolour, $7\frac{1}{2} \times 5$ ins/191 × 127 mm.
Private Collection, England.

28

to be facsimile copies. This is a common practice of artists who sell a picture and take a copy of it so that they can repeat the composition if commissioned for the same subject at a later date. Almost every work by Boys from these years, both large and small, has its copy, even such a brief sketch as *View at Swiss Cottage* (Plate 45). It is not surprising to find that later in life he reworked the subjects of this early period, and it is consistent that in his artist's sale there was one drawing dated 1832 and others undated from this same period.[27]

The many beautiful works painted by Boys during the years of 1832 and 1833 show that he had by then reached the full height of his powers. It is in the watercolours of these years that one can study Boys's own true style, now freed from the direct influence of Bonington, who had been dead for four years by this time. Bonington's style, and that of Boys before the former's death, had been young and romantic in character. In 1832 Boys was almost thirty, the youthfulness had left him, and it was natural that his watercolours should reflect this change in age.

A correspondent in *The Library of Fine Arts* described Boys in 1833 as 'too much of a mere imitator to be pleasing. He merely looks to the outward forms of his master's (Bonington's) work; he cannot dive into the intellectual qualities.'[28] It was just this type of remark that obscured the true merits of Boys's work. Other young artists such as Wyld, Cox (Figure IX), Prout (Figure XVIII), Roberts, Holland (Figure XVII) and Scarlett Davis (Figure X), basking in the reflected warmth of Bonington's success, practised much the same style; but Boys, who lived so much closer to the sun of Bonington, was obscured by its very brilliance. However, if there is one quality which the art of this early Anglo-French school did not possess, it was that of intellectualism. Their art was a spontaneous and youthful reaction to the romantic discovery of France, its Gothic and picturesque architecture, its rustic countryside, and, especially, Paris.

Paris in the 1820s was only a village compared to the vast metropolis of today. The artists wandered about in a comparatively small area and seized on the same landmarks and vistas to paint. In view of this it is not surprising to find that Boys painted the very scenes which Bonington had portrayed before him. Indeed, it would be extraordinary if it were otherwise. Boys certainly possessed watercolours by Bonington, just as the latter had owned some of Boys's (two were sold in Bonington's studio sale).[29] Even if Boys never actually copied Bonington's works, his approach to a scene must have been conditioned by seeing beforehand how Bonington had dealt with the same subject. For almost every view of Paris painted by Bonington there is a watercolour by Boys which approximates to it.

L'Institut and L'Isle de la Cité from the Quai du Louvre (Plate 27) is, for example, one of the views which Bonington had painted (Plate 24) and which Boys took up in 1833. There appears to be a curious history behind this view. Almost certainly it was originally inspired by Bonington's watercolour of the same subject; then Callow made a pencil sketch of it, on 28 and 31 May 1831, which Boys copied in a tracing-paper drawing (Plates 25 and 26). Not only are the dimensions of the two drawings similar, that by Boys is an exact tracing of Callow's version, even retaining the colour notes and the same figures at the parapet. Boys revised the drawing of the architecture at the left because it was, according to a note on Callow's drawing, 'not steep enough'. The final Boys watercolour is small in dimension and, because it is a watercolour, lacks the minute details of the larger drawing, which he has used here only to guide his general outlines and proportions. Perhaps Callow's sketch is one of those which he made for Boys and for which the latter rewarded him with books.[30] Using Callow's sketch would have saved Boys the time and trouble of drawing the scene for himself and it gave him a precise architectural framework from which he could work and improvise. The watercolour is marvellously fresh, the colours are still relatively free from fading—a fate which mars so many of his drawings from this early

IX

X

FIGURE IX **RUE VIVIENNE, PARIS,** by David Cox (1783–1859).
Watercolour, $12\frac{13}{16} \times 7\frac{1}{6}$ ins/326 × 180 mm.
Inscribed (Verso) La . . . /D. Cox: O/40
Fondation Custodia, Institut Néerlandais, Paris (1970.T.31).

FIGURE X **LE PAVILLON DE FLORE, PARIS,** by John Scarlett Davis (1804–45).
Watercolour, $8\frac{3}{16} \times 6\frac{3}{16}$ ins/208 × 157 mm.
Carnavalet Museum, Paris (D. 5866).
Photograph by Lauros-Giraudon.

30

period. The fussiness of the preparatory pencil drawings is not allowed to dominate the finished watercolour. It possesses all the qualities of a good watercolour: lightness, facility and spontaneity. It is inconceivable that this watercolour should be considered a copy in any sense of the word.

Martin Hardie[31] chastised the nineteenth-century watercolourists for being impure in their techniques. He said that the use of bodycolour, gum, scratching and washing out degraded the very qualities inherent in English watercolour. This view was somewhat doctrinaire, but understandable as soon as one looks at some of the overworked watercolours painted in imitation of oil paintings by many of the Victorian artists. This opinion has very much coloured our appreciation of nineteenth-century watercolour painting, but it is misguided when applied to a Boys of 1833. There is nothing impure about his *L'Institut from the Louvre* (Plate 27). He has sketched in the sky with quick sweeps of the brush, allowing the brilliance of the white paper to show through and so creating an almost natural radiance. The distant architecture with its economy of line forms at once a generalized tonal background as well as a true-to-life rendition. To the overall beige tint of the road are added cobbles and dust in the form of delicate and appropriate dashes of wet and dry brown scumbled over the base wash. What might have been a rather plain facade of the Louvre at the left appears to shimmer with the light, vibration and heat of the sun's rays. The side walls of the background buildings, illumined with sun, are picked out with white bodycolour. The dots of colour that distinguish the shapes of the figures form an integral part of the colour composition as well as giving a peculiarly French air to the whole scene. The dogs, delicately picked out in cool greys and browns, rush across the parched road, the only disturbance in the calm afternoon scene. Nothing is out of place or impure, the whole being more natural and true to life than the classical generalizations of a watercolour by Varley (Figure XI).

Bonington was a master of colour and spontaneous effect. Venice was the true glory of his art, and was rendered by him in alternately hot fiery watercolours and cool fluid oils; these last preview the work of Boudin in their impressionistic character. Boys mastered the same range of colours and techniques but used them to create a different style. In the works of the early 1830s he reveals himself as a master of tone. As such he is worthy to be acclaimed the successor of Girtin whose wonderful sketches of Paris were a triumph of watercolour as a tonal medium (Figure XIV). Boys must have admired him for this quality; elsewhere, in a letter, he praises him for another: 'his sketches are so correct there is not a line out'. Girtin's *Views of Paris* were nearly all of the Seine from its different bridges.[32] The plethora of views of the Seine in Paris that Boys painted between 1824 and 1832 suggest that they were painted in imitation of Girtin and may even have been for a publication to complement that of Girtin (as it was he was to conceive of a series with an essentially different character and subject matter).

The *Notre Dame* of 1832 (Plate 20) is a masterpiece of tone control: the main colouring is grey varying to white and brown, with touches of bright bodycolour. The beige of the hospital to the left is made to seem the brightest tone of the picture, and the burnt grey of the cathedral facade appears cool beside it. In turn, the darker grey of the street house on the right is cold by comparison, but itself appears warm against the white sky behind it. Each wash is carefully textured and worked at to produce just the right effect; the slightest nuance is important. The Tate Gallery's *Seine and the Palace of the Tuileries* (Plate 16) is another triumph of tone. The cool blues and greys of the buildings on the left are contrasted with the warmth of the sunlit architecture of the Tuileries on the right. These are complemented by the vaporous sky, which forms over Paris on hot days such as this was, and by the glassy, almost icy, surface of the water. Boys always painted his water in horizontal washes of dry colour, split by narrow lines of white paper

XI

XII

Figure XI **LONDON FROM GREENWICH,** by John Varley (1778–1842).
Watercolour, $5\frac{3}{4} \times 9$ ins/146 × 228 mm.
Signed (BR) J. Varley. 1835
Photograph by courtesy of the Leger Galleries, London.

FIGURE XII **MEDITERRANEAN CRAFT—GULF OF GENOA,** by Edward W. Cooke (1811–81).
Oil painting on canvas, 21 × 30 ins/533 × 762 mm.
Signed (BR) E. W. Cooke 1847
Private Collection, England.
Photograph by courtesy of the Leger Galleries, London.

32

XIII

XIV

FIGURE XIII **PARIS FROM THE PONT DES ARTS,** by William Callow (1812–1908).
Watercolour, $13\frac{1}{2} \times 19\frac{1}{2}$ ins/343 × 495 mm.
Signed (BR) W. Callow
Private Collection, England.

FIGURE XIV **RUE ST DENIS,** by Thomas Girtin (1775–1802).
Watercolour, $9 \times 19\frac{1}{4}$ ins/228 × 489 mm.
Tate Gallery, London (T.990).

scratched out with a knife to give an effect of recession and texture. The whiteness of the paper showing through the dragged washes contributes to the creation of the surface brilliance of the water.

The precision, control and concentration of these three watercolours is a phenomenon that Bonington could never have achieved. They have a sense of permanence and inevitability which Bonington's more ephemeral and capricious art never encompassed. However, they do not possess the high-keyed colouring of Bonington's watercolours, which virtually assault the visual senses. Nevertheless, Boys was also capable of highly coloured work. *Paris from Bercy* (Plate 32) seems rich in colour with its orange and veridian contrasts, but the appearance belies the facts; Boys has keyed up the tone of the picture without increasing the richness of his colours. The same range of beiges, sepias and browns appear in this watercolour as in his others. To create the impression of a sunset evening he has bathed the whole in an orange glow skilfully achieved without the actual use of orange (except on the base of the folly where it is almost cool in effect). There are two small sketches by Boys,[33] undated, but unquestionably from this early period, which display a greater range of colour with pinks, blues, greens, aquamarines, yellows and oranges, all of which are tinted tonally. One is bathed in a smooth wash of gum which deepens its colours, and both are worked and textured according to his usual watercolour technique. In these pictures Boys has employed bright colours, but, paradoxically, he has skilfully keyed down the brightness by tinting them all harmoniously and tonally.

Boys also painted watercolours which by comparison seem sombre and dull in their range of colour, but which have much merit. *Le Pont Royal et la cour des Comptes en construction* (1833)[34] portrays a day very different from that in the Tate Gallery's sun-filled view of the Seine, and from that evening warmth of *Paris from Bercy*. Here is a relatively cool and blustery day: the colours of the picture are bleak greens, blues and grey-browns, relieved by pin-prick dots of scarlet and sky-blue which betray the presence of people. The dark shadows predominate and the shapes of the trees form menacing masses, but even so Boys manages to create space and luminosity, which give the picture its grandeur.

All the watercolours discussed above have been of French or Parisian scenes; nevertheless Boys, while resident in Paris in the early 1830s, made several short trips to England. The few watercolours that he made on these visits are mostly of London or Greenwich, although he did make excursions to Chester (Plates 35 and 36) and York (Plates 37 and 38). The Greenwich scenes (Plates 33 and 34) are essentially rural and, in particular, show Boys's mastery of foliage. The trees are mostly seen in terms of mass rather than lines; however, he indicates the foliage by quickly sketched branches and the leaves by varied brushwork. He uses his fingers to give texture to the washes and scratches out the colour to let the paper show through. This creates the feeling of airiness and freedom which is the keynote of these scenes. The total effect of this treatment, together with the range of cool greens and beige-oranges, gives an English flavour to the pictures which is distinct from the mood of his French watercolours.

Most of these early watercolours, while being modest in size, give the impression of being much larger. It is one of Boys's failings that he tended to lose the superb control over his colours and tones that he shows in these small-scale pictures when he attempted larger works. The *Place Louis XV* in the Bibliothèque Nationale fails as a picture.[35] The touches and techniques which he related so well in his smaller pictures do not form any sort of harmony here. Indeed, the foreground figure with the dogs appears to be falling over backwards! *The Louvre and the Pont des Arts,*[36] a picture of mammoth proportions, is unsuccessful for similar reasons and merely looks awkward and laboured. His large-scale exhibition works may well have suffered from this same mediocrity which in turn would have been detrimental to his ambitions as a watercolourist during this period.

Little is known about the preliminary working methods which Boys used for painting his watercolours of the early 1830s, chiefly due to the fact that there are no sketch books in existence. However, there are various pencil drawings by Boys which indicate that he used two very different drawing techniques; the first is freehand, as shown in the *Pont Royal from the Institute* (Plate 21). The lines are rough, uneven and lack precision—although the essential details are well rendered; he draws the column capitals in a larger scale so that he can paint them correctly in the finished watercolour (Plate 22). It is simply an outline drawing with the minimum of shading. The figures, briefly sketched, are placed on top of the architectural drawing. He records the wording of the placards on the windows, always a feature of his work. The second drawing style is demonstrated by the *Pont Royal and the Quai d'Orsay* (Plate 23), more or less from the opposite side of the Pont Royal. It has the same character of an outline drawing with the minimum of shading and with the figures sketched over the architecture, but the absolute precision makes it completely different and almost inartistic.

This stylistic discrepancy could be explained by the use of the Graphic Telescope, invented by Cornelius Varley in 1811.[37] The Telescope reflected the view down onto a piece of paper and enabled the artist to draw outlines of the scene in front of him. It was used by many artists and printers alike (the latter used it for reducing drawings for engraving). It is known that Cotman used one on his 1817 tour of Normandy and E. W. Cooke used it for sketching ships at Portsmouth in 1831 and probably to draw plants for *Loddiges' Botanical Cabinet*. Boys was a close friend of E. W. Cooke and worked on the *Botanical Cabinet* with him before 1833. It is reasonable to assume that Boys knew of its existence if he had not actually used it. The Telescope had a wide-angle lens and gave just the sort of viewpoint obtained by Boys in this drawing (Plate 23). The wide expanse of foreground, though curiously attractive, is inartistic and the whole appearance of the drawing is mechanical. It is possible that Boys also used the Telescope for his engravings.

When examined, the underdrawing in the watercolours described above is extremely thin and generalized. It has neither the detail nor the precision of either of his two drawing styles. Probably he only used his drawings to give him the general proportions and features of his watercolours, and so drew the outlines very briefly. He laid his washes of colour over this under-drawing and finally worked in the detail and precision of the drawings with sepia or grey-brown on the tip of his brush. The drawings thus served two functions: one was to provide the guidelines of the composition, the other was to ensure the accuracy of his architectural detail in the appearance of the finished watercolour—a mixture of freedom and exactitude that is peculiar to Boys.

What is not provided for in this process is one very important element—colour. It is odd that there are no very brief colour sketches which would supply the connecting link. Some of his drawings are annotated with colour notes, but that would hardly have sufficed.[38] Did he colour his drawings on the spot, thus invalidating the need for colour sketches? The colour in some of his watercolours is so fresh, the tones so true and balanced, the air so light and natural that it is inconceivable that they were done inside a studio. He made second versions of many of his views, and these often have the appearance of *plein-air* drawings (Plates 33 and 46), and sometimes of copies lacking in flair and familiarity with the subject. If the former were mostly studio-executed, how much more his sense of colour and life is to be admired. However, it is impossible to state, for lack of evidence, the extent to which Boys worked in front of his subject.

One aspect of his methods that is brought out by these drawings, and will be discussed later in relation to his lithographs, is his system of treating his architecture and his figures as independent. In his finished watercolours his figures are almost always different from their appearance in his drawings (Plates 21 and 22), and in successive versions of the same watercolour he invariably changes the disposition of the figures (Plates 45 and 46). He treats his pictures rather like stages in a theatre. The stationary backcloth and stage are formed by the architecture and the ground, against which he then proceeded to move his figures around like actors. This stark division of the picture into components reveals a dispassionate interest in overall design, not to say a rare capability for imagining and inventing figural compositions. The figures in Bonington's water-colours are always part of the original scene, in other words they were there when he drew or painted it. Boys's are different—their *raison d'être* is purely for compositional effect irrespective of what was actually in front of him. In addition they provide touches of character and humour without which any watercolour by Boys would be the poorer.

In his own letters Boys reveals little to throw light on his methods. However, there are one or two remarks which may illuminate our understanding. In his letter of 1833[39] he refers to Girtin's sketch as being 'so correct that there is not a line out'; the tone of this implies that he regarded it as a challenge to do better. In the same letter he criticizes other artists' work for being 'incorrect', and that he himself wants to do 'Paris *as* it is'. To achieve the precision to outdo Girtin, the Graphic Telescope would have been invaluable. 'I tear up a good many'[40] he also said about his drawings for a certain project for which he was commissioned. It is not known what this com-mission was, but his words give some indication of the care and time he took to produce a work of art. This may account for the scarcity of his watercolours and may also explain the absence of sketch books and drawings.[41] His practice of dividing up his pictures into components—sketch and precision, outline and tone/colour, figures and architecture—is especially interesting and must surely stem from his engraving and lithographic methods, which had a strong effect on his watercolour style. It was to lithography that Boys turned his attention more and more after 1833.

NOTES TO CHAPTER TWO

1 *Familia Boisiana*, British Museum MS Add 45500.
2 *The Morning Chronicle*, 21 February 1834.
3 *The Magazine of Fine Arts*, 1833, page 143.
4 *Ibid.*, page 149.
5 William Callow, *Autobiography*, ed. H.M. Cundall, London, 1908, Chapter III, page 12.
6 Perhaps Callow had some personal motive which prompted him to make this remark. We cannot rule out the possibility that Callow might have felt jealous of Boys's close relationship with Bonington.
7 La Bibliothèque d'Art et d'Archéologie, Paris. The letter has a series of doodles drawn on it, presumably by Boys. Baron Rivet was an amateur artist in his own right. Auguste was a friend of Delacroix and Géricault and shared their interest in the Orient.
8 *R. P. Bonington: his life and work*, by A. Dubuisson and C. E. Hughes, London, 1924, Chapter IX, page 84.
9 Undated and unaddressed letter in the Henry E. Huntington Library and Art Gallery, San Marino, California (H.M. 16679).
10 *Watercolour Painting in Britain*, by Martin Hardie, London, 1967; Volume II: *The Romantic Period*, Chapter 11, page 185.
11 I refer the reader to Dr Marion Spencer's *Catalogue Raisonné*, currently in preparation.
12 Carnavalet Museum, Paris (D. 5871). There also exists a sepia wash and pen sketch of the same, $9\frac{1}{8} \times 5\frac{9}{16}$ ins/ 232×141 mm., inscribed (BC) *Fountain of Pity*, verso pencil sketches of the Porte Rouge, Notre Dame (later Plate XVI in *Picturesque Architecture*, 1839) inscribed *Bouchez/Maitre d'Armes/Rue St Jacques No. 118, White and Black letters*. With the Albany Gallery, London, 1974. This attribution must remain tentative until more of Boys's early sketches have come to light.
13 Victoria and Albert Museum, London (A.L. 5745). (Frontispiece.) Also see Plate 53.
14 In the collection of Mr and Mrs Paul Mellon.
15 Callow, *op cit.*, pages 18–19.

16 Letter of 17 August 1831, written from 33 Avenue de Neuilly, Paris, to Henry Mogford at 45 Newington Place, Kennington Common, London; in the Henry E. Huntington Library and Art Gallery, San Marino, California (H.M. 16680).

17 Letter of 9 September 1833, written from 19 Rue du Bouloy, Paris, to Henry Mogford c/o Monsr. Montenais, Pensionnât, à Marquise près Boulogne-sur-Mer; in the Henry E. Huntington Library and Art Gallery, San Marino, California (H.M. 16681).

18 *Ibid.*

19 E. W. Cooke's diaries are in the possession of Mr C. R. Cooke, O.B.E. and were kindly shown to me by Mr John Munday of the National Maritime Museum, Greenwich.

20 Callow, *op. cit.,* page 18.

21 'Edward Webb (1805–1854) an artist and his journals', by Denis Thomas, published in *The Connoisseur,* March 1973, page 105.

22 Letter cited.

23 *Ibid.*

24 No. 19 Rue du Bouloy is only a stone's throw from the Louvre, and was thus very centrally placed.

25 Callow, *op. cit.,* pages 21–22.

26 The *Dictionary of National Biography* states that Poynter was a pupil of Boys before 1819, which is impossible. A far more likely date is 1832.

27 The artist's sale was held, presumably after his death, at 30 Acacia Road, St John's Wood, in the house in which he died. The drawing is of *Père la Chaise,* and is dated 1832; now in a Private Collection, England.

28 *Library of Fine Arts,* 1833, page 149.

29 Two watercolours by Boys were sold at the disposal of Bonington's studio effects at Sotheby on 10 February 1838: Lots 66 and 77, they were respectively a *View on the French coast* and a *View near Rouen.*

30 Callow, *op. cit.,* page 18.

31 Hardie, *op. cit.,* Volumes II and III passim.

32 *A Selection of Twenty of the most Picturesque Views in Paris,* London, 1803.

33 *Landscape with Windmill* (sunset in the fields), watercolour, $3\frac{3}{8} \times 4\frac{3}{4}$ ins/86 × 121 mm., signed (CB) *T.B.,* British Museum, London (1884.4.25.1). *Landscape with river and figures,* watercolour, $2\frac{5}{8} \times 6$ ins/67 × 152 mm., Private Collection, England.

34 Carnavalet Museum, Paris (D. 5867).

35 Watercolour, $14\frac{1}{2} \times 23\frac{1}{2}$ ins/368 × 597 mm., Bibliothèque Nationale, Paris (Ve.53.h.1061).

36 Watercolour, $25\frac{3}{8} \times 40\frac{9}{16}$/645 × 1030 mm., signed (BR) *T. S. Boys,* Louvre, Paris (RF.35.728).

37 See Michael Pidgley, 'Cornelius Varley, Cotman, and the Graphic Telescope', *The Burlington Magazine,* CXIV, 1972, page 785.

38 See, for example, some of the tracing paper drawings in the British Museum album (1952.5.10.9.35).

39 Letter cited.

40 Letter of 1831, cited.

41 Recently three leaves from a sketchbook by Boys have come to light. They all depict, in watercolour, English canal and river scenes. One represents a stormy landscape, $3\frac{5}{8} \times 6$ ins/92 × 152 mm., and is signed *T.S. Boys* and inscribed *In April* (?). Presumably they were made on a sketching tour in England, possibly during the 1840s or '50s. The treatment is light and sketchy catching the essence of each scene in broad wet strokes of colour. On the verso of one leaf there are studies of canal barges and cows, and on another the steps of a country house.

III
LITHOGRAPHY

THE Revolution and the subsequent Napoleonic Wars took their toll of France in many ways. Not surprisingly, the nation's artists shared in the suffering: many were killed during this period, and many more found it difficult to operate because of a lack of social and economic security. The French art establishment had little to offer other than the teaching of such old men as Baron Antoine Gros, in whose atelier Bonington worked. The engraving profession suffered a similar decline and there was little activity during the first thirty years of the century; this in turn provided good opportunities for foreigners such as Engelmann, Hullmandel, Arrowsmith, Senefelder and Ostervald, to name only a few. The large publications of such patrons as Mazois, Hittorff, Gau, Denon and Zanth during the early part of the century were engraved by a relatively small number of artists. The names Dormier, Baltar, Bigan, Baltard, Hibou, Nyon, Sellier, Frommel, Bishop, Hamilton,[1] Clara Adams and, later, Boys crop up with great regularity. The influx of young foreign printers and engravers is understandable.[2] Boys, with his qualification of an apprenticeship under the revered George Cooke, must have been very welcome.

While he was in Paris, he maintained his contacts with the Cooke family, and just as they invited him to work on Loddige's *Botanical Cabinet* on his return visits to London so he, in return, gave work to them.[3] The Bibliothèque Nationale possesses two versions of an engraving of *Paris and the Louvre from the Pont des Arts,* close in composition to Boys's Tate Gallery watercolour of the same (Plate 16). This was engraved by W. Cooke (presumably W. J., Boys's brother-in-law).

A detailed study has yet to be made of the connections between the English and French schools at this time, but Boys was surely a very important link. Many of the works which he engraved were issued on both sides of the Channel.[4] E. W. Cooke's diaries show that Boys brought over M. Bovinet, the French publisher, in March of 1830.[5] It is no coincidence that Boys was back in England in June and July 1834, when Cooke tells of meetings between Baron Taylor, M. Dauzats, Louis Haghe and his brother, who had all come to England, and Hullmandel, Harding, Gale, Damard and others (including himself).[6] In November of the same year E. W. and W.J. Cooke corresponded with Baron Taylor.[7] It is possible that it was Boys who made these arrangements and who introduced the Frenchmen to the Cooke family. Furthermore, it was Boys who introduced both Callow[8] and William Wyld[9] to E. W. Cooke. Boys's studio in the Rue du Bouloy was a meeting-place for many distinguished English artists travelling through France; Callow tells of men such as Samuel Prout[10] and John Lewis[11] visiting Boys's atelier. The culmination of these Anglo-French connections was the *Voyages Pittoresques* of Baron Taylor, on which every English draughtsman and lithographer of merit was employed.

It must have been in Paris that Boys learnt the art of lithography. It was certainly not practised in Cooke's studio; in any case the latter strongly disapproved of steel engraving and so it is likely that he would have been horrified at the thought of lithography, a recent invention.[12] It is not known in which studio Boys learnt the technique. Motte, Delpech and Engelmann are all likely sources, as of course is Bonington who also practised it. Bonington, however, does not appear to have concerned himself more than superficially with lithography. His lithographs lack the clarity and subtle texturing of tones that are the true properties of this printing process (Figure XV). Since Boys was an engraver by trade, he is likely to have interested himself in this new technique at an early stage, although his first published lithograph did not appear until 1832.[13]

John Saddler's letter (see pages 21–22) about the last sketches ever made by Bonington in W. J. Cooke's studio shows that Boys was keen to experiment. On that occasion Boys was trying out a new type of permanent brown ink extracted from the shells of walnuts. Callow also related how he 'learnt a good deal of the theory and practice of art from Boys'.[14] Perhaps this experimental side of Boys's character is what Callow and others were referring to when they called him eccentric; certainly he was clever, and quick to exploit new techniques. In this context there is a strong possibility that he used the Graphic Telescope. In the early 1830s he also experimented with soft-ground etchings of which five examples are known,[15] but they were never published and were presumably made to satisfy his own curiosity about the medium (Plate 39).

Compared with his later lithographic work the early engravings which Boys made for the large French topographical books on ancient ruins are mundane in appearance.[16] He adapted himself to fit into the required style which was rather dry and linear. Executed after other artists' drawings, they are competent pieces of engraving but no more. He could hardly have displayed great or technical virtuosity through these rather limited commissions. It was probably because of the lack of opportunities presented by this bread-and-butter engraving work that he decided to experiment with other techniques. His lithograph of the *Château de Laeken* contains elements daring for what may have been his first published lithograph: it attempts to portray the wet surfaces of the roads and buildings just after a thunderstorm; Boys even adds a rainbow over the Château at the right. Well drawn and executed, it is evidently not the work of a new-comer to the medium.

.His next lithographs were for the *Voyages Pittoresques* of Baron Taylor, the magnum opus of French nineteenth-century topography. Boys had become associated with Baron Taylor at an early stage in his lithographic career, and the Baron commissioned from Boys twenty-four lithographs between 1833 and 1845.[17] In this work the progress of lithography is portrayed from its infancy in 1820 through its maturity in the 1840s to the decline in quality of the 1850s and later. The *Voyages Pittoresques* also provided Boys with the means of proving his capabilities in the new medium.

Although the effect of lithography is akin to simple pencil drawings, the artist has to learn the technique fully before he can produce a lithograph of quality. The process is complicated to explain, but to understand Boys's practice it is necessary that the reader should understand its basic precepts.

> The art of lithography depends upon a very simple principle, viz: the attraction which calcareous stone has for water and greasy substances, and the want of affinity between the two latter.[18]

The artist draws with a lithographic crayon (consisting of wax-soap and lamp black) upon a prepared stone. The drawing is fixed with acid, bathed in water—which the wax repels—then coated with lithographic printing ink which clings to the wax drawing and is repelled by the damp surface of the stone. Next, in the printing process, paper is placed carefully on the stone and run through the press, after which the stone is washed clean (the drawing stays fixed on); this procedure is repeated for each impression. The drawing prints in reverse, and great skill is needed in the drawing and the subsequent build-up of tones or shaded areas. The delicacy of the chemical printing processes requires that no mistakes are made, for it is easy to spoil the surface of the stone with clumsy handling.

XV

XVI

XV

FIGURE XV **RUE DU GROS-HORLOGE, ROUEN,** by Richard Parkes Bonington (1803–28).
Lithograph, 10¼ × 9⅞ ins/261 × 251 mm.
Plate in *Voyages Pittoresques et Romantiques dans l'Ancienne France, Ancienne Normandie,* Paris, 1825.
Victoria and Albert Museum, London (E.512–1910).
Photograph by courtesy of The Paul Mellon Centre for Studies in British Art, London.

FIGURE XVI **ROUEN,** by Richard Parkes Bonington (1803–28).
Watercolour, 7⅛ × 9⅛ ins/181 × 232 mm.
The Wallace Collection, London.
Reproduced by permission of the Trustees of the Wallace Collection.

FIGURE XVII **RUE DU GROS-HORLOGE, ROUEN,** by James Holland (1799–1870).
Pencil and wash, 18 × 12 ins/457 × 305 mm.
Inscribed (BL) <u>ROUEN/Augt 14th</u>
      (On the wall at R) ½ <u>light</u>
Victoria and Albert Museum, London (P.25–1968).
Reproduced by courtesy of the Victoria and Albert Museum.

40

Lithography approaches more closely than any other printing process to the quality of an original pencil drawing. The artist is able to build up a tonal area by careful cross-hatching with the lithographic crayon. The range of intermediate tones is great. Further, the artist can use the graining of the stone to lighten his shading, analogous in a pencil drawing to using the roughness of the paper. By skilful work, the artist can build up a wide range of tones and textures, more than in other printing processes.[19] In his watercolours Boys had already revealed his qualities as a tonal draughtsman; he was thus well suited to exploit the true properties of lithography to which he turned at the height of his powers as an artist.

There are watercolours relating to some but not all of his lithographs, and those that do sometimes vary greatly in composition and treatment. The detail required for a lithograph such as *Place du Grand Marché d'Abbeville* (Plate 41) could not have been provided by a watercolour. The existence of a large quantity of red chalk on tracing-paper drawings,[20] mostly relating to his lithographs, provides a clue to the preparatory work Boys did for a lithograph. Most are exactly the same size as the corresponding lithographs, and are similar in detail. It is reasonable to assume that these are direct tracings from drawings or watercolours made by Boys, also that their specific purpose was for transferring the outline from the drawing or watercolour onto the lithographic stone. The tracing-paper drawing would be placed face down on the stone and pulled through the press so that the lines of the drawing would show faintly, in reverse, on the surface of the stone. With the aid of a mirror the artist was then able to build up his tones and details from the guidelines provided by this transfer process. For Plate XV of *Stanfield's Sketches on the Meuse*[21] (for which Boys did the lithographs) there exists a straightforward tracing drawing taken directly from Stanfield's drawing without alteration. It has the halting line characteristic of a tracing.[22] The drawings relating to Roberts's *Picturesque Sketches of Spain* (1837) are of similar character.[23] This was the accepted method by which a lithographic engraver reproduced his own or another artist's drawing.

It appears that a quantity of the tracing-paper drawings relating to the *London as it is* series were actually sketched from nature; drawings for the Frontispiece and Plate VII are inscribed respectively: *sketched 8.4.1840* and *sketched 22.4.1840*.[24] Others bear pencil instructions and colour notes. Possibly they were sketched with the aid of the Graphic Telescope like the preparatory drawings for his watercolours (Plate 23). Most of the tracing drawings in the British Museum relate to his *Picturesque Architecture in Paris* series. In those representing *Notre Dame de Paris, Hôtel de Sens, Paris* (Plate 52A) and the *Rue de la Grosse Horloge, Rouen*,[25] the architectural details appear to have been traced, and are reproduced exactly in the final lithographs. However, the figural compositions are completely different; the figures in the foreground differ from those in the final lithographs. Assuming that Boys transferred the architecture of these tracing drawings straight onto the lithographic stone, the figures must have been added to the tracings subsequently. They are freehand in character, the positions of some have been changed and overdrawn with pencil. It seems that they are experiments for the figure compositions of the final lithographs. In his watercolours he had regarded the figures as moveable props, as opposed to the stationary architectural 'stage', and it is not surprising therefore to find him repeating this for his lithographs. It indicates a cross-fertilization between the different disciplines, and a movement towards the creation of a single all-embracing working method for producing watercolours and lithographs alike.

It is not proven that Boys used this technique as early as 1833. His first contribution to the *Voyages Pittoresques—La Grande Rue de Cordes—*is relatively pedestrian and shows no special skill in handling.[26] However, a drawing on tracing-paper exists for it in the British Museum which suggests that he may have been using part of the above method even at this early date.[27] For his subsequent lithographs in the *Voyages Pittoresques* no tracing-paper drawings exist. Boys's contribution to this series reflects the development of lithography during the 1830s. From his first hesitant beginnings he moves on to show how well he was able to adapt his art to lithography. It was through the *Voyages Pittoresques* that he first met Charles Hullmandel, the man who was so dedicated to improving lithographic techniques. This early relationship emphasizes the Anglo-French connection whereby an English artist working in France had his lithographs for a French publication printed in England. The two views of Abbeville (Plates 40 and 41) show the early maturity Boys attained in this medium; there are no inconsistencies or weaknesses of drawing, and the handling of tones, their contrasts and juxtapositions, is expert. The country has a relaxed and pastoral feeling. The meandering course of the river in this view is very much a *voyage pittoresque* for the viewer. By contrast, the market place is a dramatic build-up of forms, tones and lights; the shadowed and sunlit parts are cleverly differentiated in the composition and disposition of the buildings. The character of this afternoon provincial market scene is rendered with precision and economy. In both cases he uses the sandy granular texture of the lithographic stone to advantage in creating even and rich tonal areas. Here Boys shows that he had mastered the techniques of producing the basic lithographic qualities of line and tone.

At the same time he was also working on *Architecture pittoresque dessinée d'après nature*, 1835.[28] This was produced in conjunction with Adolphe Rouargue and was printed by Delpech in Paris. The character of a lithograph depends to a great extent on the printer, and it is interesting to compare here the lithographs by Boys printed in England with those printed in France. In Hullmandel's lithograph (Plate 41) the use of the graining of the stone is subordinate to the tones; whereas in Delpech's (Plate 43) it is more apparent throughout the picture and gives it a much lighter character. The artificial effect of the graining in fact makes the views much more picturesque, as if seen through a haze. The contrasts between light and dark are much less in Delpech's print and reveal a comparatively limited range. But however satisfying this effect may be to the eye, it certainly shows the essential difference in character between the English and French styles of lithographic printing, as exemplified respectively by Hullmandel and Delpech. This difference was perhaps due as much to individual as to national preferences: very simply, each printer differed from every other.

The view of *L'Eglise de l'Abbaye de Maguelonne* in the *Voyages Pittoresques* (Plate 44) reveals developments in Boys's technique, and provides an interesting comparison with a view of the same subject by a French artist; for Baron Taylor included two identical views next to each other—an act of rare extravagance. Adrien Dauzats drew the other, which differs only in minor details but does not have the same precision as that by Boys and may have been taken from the latter's view; it is also slightly smaller in extent. Apparently the church was disused, so the introduction by Boys of a monk praying is a rather romantic and imaginative feature. In his lithograph the graining of the stone is even finer than before; the effect of the picture rests on the delicate tonal movement from the sunlit walls to the deepest recesses of the chapel. In his previous lithographs the light areas were achieved by leaving the paper to show through and not drawing on them. Here, Boys renders some of the lights by scratching away his drawing. The whites produced thus are much sharper and are particularly effective as, literally, pinpricks of light flickering on the edges of the blocks of masonry. Boys himself in a letter to *The Probe* on 10 January 1840 gives an account of this very procedure:

> I produce . . . the masses of light, by what is termed by aqua-tint engravers, brush-biting, that is, laying on to the ground work of chalk or ink, weak acid, and with a camel's hair pencil [drawing] where I want light; thus positively . . . scraping in the forms of the whites.

The effect of this is analogous in watercolour to scraping out whites with a knife or a wet cloth, as Boys does in the pilasters of the Louvre and in the dog in his *Pavillon de Flore* (Plate 53). It illustrates the close correspondence between his watercolours and his lithographs (although this particular method in watercolours was widely used by this time).

This view of the Abbey at Maguelonne (Plate 44) also displays a new departure in the development of lithography—the use of lithographic washes on the stone to supplement the drawing. This was developed at roughly the same time, *circa* 1836, in both France and England by Engelmann and Hullmandel respectively. The former calls it 'lavis lithographique',[29] the latter the 'dabbing style'. Basically, it consisted of using a circular wooden implement, stuffed with cotton and covered with kid skin, which was charged with lithographic ink and applied to the surface of the stone in a series of 'dabbings'. Its effect was to build up an even tone over a large area in a relatively short time. Boys used Hullmandel's development in various of his contributions to the *Voyages Pittoresques,* for example the *Angle Sud Est dans l'Intérieur des Remparts à Aigues-Mortes.*[30] However, in the Maguelonne view there is evidence of a further extension of the process called lithotint, another step towards the imitation of watercolours. James Duffield Harding was its main exponent; it can be seen to advantage in his *Sketches at Home and Abroad*[31] as an independent technique. Here Boys uses it purely in a supplementary fashion to give fluidity and depth to the darkest areas. The ink has the appearance of having been brushed on and adds resonance to the shadows of the chapel and the folds of the monk's habit. It is not particularly daring, but it does exhibit Boys's involvement with the very latest developments of lithography. Hullmandel did not even patent the process until 5 November 1840.

Until 1837 Boys had worked mostly in France, but, as Ottley records, it was '1837 when he was recalled to England to lithograph the works of David Roberts and Clarkson Stanfield'.[32] It is not known whether it was expressly to do these works that he returned; it is possible that he was soured by his progress in France and wished to return to his native country which offered better opportunities. On his return he was employed first of all by David Roberts,[33] then by Clarkson Stanfield[34] and George Vivian.[35] In these publications Boys uses another lithographic invention—the tint stone, invented by Hullmandel and Harding. Lithographs were felt to lack body and thus the idea of printing a basic colour with the addition of another stone was introduced, analogous in watercolours to using tinted paper. The one outstanding characteristic of all these lithographs is that they reflect the individual styles of Roberts, Stanfield and Vivian rather than that of Boys. His own personality is not found in the prints and Boys reveals himself as a faithful and just reproductive lithographer.

It should not be thought that Boys gave up his involvement with other printing processes during the 1830s. As late as 1838 Mazois and Gau's *Ruines de Pompée*[36] included three etchings by Boys. Nevertheless it is clear that his attention was turned almost fully towards lithography. His watercolour painting also suffered a decline through his involvement with this medium. After 1833 there are only a handful of dated works each year which tail off even more towards 1839, the year of his *Picturesque Architecture in Paris* series. Boys may also have been painting in oils during this period as he exhibited one—*Greenwich, from Observatory Hill*—at the Society of British Artists in Suffolk Street in 1838.[37] It is paradoxical that, whereas his own watercolour production should be declining in favour of his preoccupation with lithography, the main aim of lithography during the 1830s was the imitation of watercolours. Every invention was a further step in this direction. There was great cross-fertilization between the two techniques and Boys as an exponent of both was well qualified to be in the vanguard of this development.

1 George Hamilton engraved two of Boys's drawings for Commodore Robert Elliot's *Views in India, China and on the Shores of the Red Sea*, London, 1835. This was published in London by Fisher, Son & Co., see Gustave von Groschwitz's *Prints of Thomas Shotter Boys* (essay in *Prints*, ed. C. Zigrosser, London, 1963, pages 191–215, Check List No. 12).

2 I am indebted to Dr Jean Adhémar for his observations on the state of French engraving during the 1820s.

3 Two plates in *Architecture moderne de la Sicilie etc.*, by Hittorff and Zanth (published 1835 in Paris by Paul Renouard), for which Boys executed two plates, are engraved by C. G. Cooke (presumably George Cooke) and E. G. Cooke (E. W. Cooke). Boys must have obtained this work for them. George Cooke died in February 1833, so the engraving must have been done before that date.

4 Some examples are *Views in India, op. cit.*, and the *Voyages Pittoresques et romantiques dans l'ancienne France*, by Charles Nodier, J. Taylor, and Alphonse de Cailleux. 19 volumes, Paris, 1820–78.

5 *Op. cit.*, 15 and 30 March.

6 *Ibid.*, 24 and 28 June.

7 *Ibid.*

8 Callow, *op. cit.*, page 22.

9 Cooke, *op. cit.*, 15 September 1832.

10 Callow, *op. cit.*, page 22.

11 *Ibid.*, page 24.

12 I refer the reader to *Lithography 1800–1850*, by M. L. Twyman, London, 1950, for a recent and informed account of the invention and early practice of lithography, and for a detailed description of its techniques.

13 This was *Château de Laeken*, $7\frac{3}{16} \times 9\frac{13}{16}$ ins/187 × 249 mm., signed (BL) *T. Boys 1832* in reverse; printed by Delpech.

14 Callow, *op. cit.*, page 18.

15 Groschwitz, *op. cit.*, Check List Nos. 6, 8, 9 and 10. Also *Le Café Momus et la Rue des Prêtres St Germain l'Auxerrois, Paris,* in the Metropolitan Museum of Art, New York (10028). Preliminary drawings on tracing paper exist for these soft-ground etchings. The relevant drawing for *Le Café Momus* in the Carnavalet Museum (D. 167) bears a partly illegible inscription, possibly '*1829*'.

16 *Architecture antique de la Sicilie etc.* by J. Hittorff (published monthly from May 1827 by Paul Renouard in Paris) for which Boys etched four plates.

17 Groschwitz, *op. cit.*, Check List No. 13.

18 *Colour Printing and Colour Printers* by R. M. Burch, London, 1910, page 174. See also Note 12 above.

19 Lithography at that early stage was no quick and easy process; a consistent tone had to be built up painstakingly over a matter of days rather than of minutes.

20 Album in the British Museum, London (1952.5.10.9.35) and some two hundred drawings in a private collection in America.

21 Published in 1838; Groschwitz, *op, cit.*, Check List No. 20.

22 British Museum, London (1952.5.10.10).

23 Private collection in America.

24 *Ibid.*

25 British Museum, London (1952.5.10.17, 15 and 13).

26 *Languedoc,* Volume I, Part 1, vignette for folio 3, page 1.

27 British Museum, London (1952.5.10.24).

28 Groschwitz, *op. cit.*, Check List No. 15.

29 Engelmann first thought of this in 1819, and patented the idea on 27 October of that year.

30 *Languedoc,* Volume II, Part 2, Plate 297 bis.

31 Published in 1840, printed by Hullmandel.

32 Ottley, *op. cit.*

33 Roberts, *op. cit.*

34 Stanfield, *op. cit.*

35 *Spanish Scenery,* London, 1838, and *Scenery of Portugal and Spain,* London, 1839; Groschwitz, *op. cit.*, Check List Nos. 21 and 22.

36 Paris, 1838, printed by Firmin Didot; Groschwitz, *op. cit.*, Check List No. 19.

37 See Appendix B. Boys's style in oil painting is still obscure. There exist many oil paintings which have been attributed to him, but without any fundamental conception of his style as an oil painter it is difficult to accept them without any supporting documentation. Boys has been a convenient label for a mediocre oil painting dating from around the 1830s. It is known that he painted oil paintings, but probably not very many. He exhibited two at the Society of British Artists in 1830. Evidently Stokes was lucky enough to be able to inspect a number of oil paintings attributed to Boys for he records: 'Boys was not at comfort in this method. The few oils by Boys that have come under examination are careful, but dull. They lack sparkle and vivacity. His coast scenes recall the works of Collins and Cooke [Figure 12]. His oils—whether of landscape, sea or town— lack the exquisite depth and atmosphere which are the signatures of every canvas from the hand of Bonington.' 'T. S. Boys', by Hugh Stokes, article in *Walker's Quarterly*, No. 18, London, 1926.

IV
INVENTION & RECOGNITION

THE direction and ambitions of Boys's work in lithography during the 1830s were consummated in 1839 with the publication of his *Picturesque Architecture in Paris, Ghent, Rouen, etc.* These ambitions had been thwarted while he had lived in Paris, partly due to the fact that he himself was not French. The French publishers were unwilling to publish a work exclusively by a foreign artist. His relations with the French publishers were not good in 1833[1] and it does not seem that they improved; it was to England that he next turned, where his cousin, Thomas Boys, had become a successful publisher with Messrs Moon, Boys and Graves before starting up his own business in Golden Square, Soho. The relatively wealthy Thomas Boys was prepared to help his artist cousin realize his long-held ambition to produce his own series of lithographs.

From his early apprentice days in George Cooke's studio, where large topographical works were being engraved every day, Shotter Boys must always have wanted to produce something comparable. During the late 1820s and early 1830s he had built up his watercolour style and had kept abreast of the latest techniques in lithography, and was thoroughly acquainted with the intricacies of the process. Artistically, he was ready to produce his own work. He had decided as early as 1833 that this series was going to depict Paris and he saw it as succeeding and complementing Girtin's series of aquatints on Paris:

> I have a folio full of good material. I am about a work on Paris to follow up Girtin's, for it has never been done by him & his sketches are so correct there is not a line out. Nash's, Batty's, Pugin's, Skelton's & all the French (excepting the beautiful Silvestre's which are not always correct) are the damndest, lying, ill got up, money getting clap trap possible. I intend to do 'Paris *as it is*' & I flatter myself I have some picturesque bits but I am soured with publishers so must do it myself.[2]

He must have tried to do this series while he was resident in Paris, but there was no one who was prepared to aid him. In his cousin he found a ready and well-to-do sponsor who was moreover a printer and would have allowed Shotter Boys more scope than any other publisher might have done.

From the extract quoted above it is clear that Boys had conceived of the series in principle by 1833 and already possessed material in the form of watercolours and drawings from which he could execute his lithographs. It is unlikely that he returned to Paris in 1838 or 1839 to make further drawings for the series, for he would have relied upon his 'folio of good material'. It was was from these watercolours and drawings, dating mostly from the early 1830s, that he made his orange chalk tracing-paper drawings[3] which were preliminaries to the lithographs. It is in these tracing-paper drawings that Boys finally worked out his compositions; the architectural details were traced from some previous watercolour or drawing over which the figural details were improvised. The fact that surprisingly few watercolours exist which relate directly to the Paris lithographs suggests that Boys may have relied predominantly on drawings; in his desire to be correct it is unlikely that watercolours alone could have provided the requisite accuracy.

The view of the *Hôtel de Sens,* mentioned in connection with Boys's earlier series of *Architecture pittoresque dessinée d'après nature* (Plate 50) appears again in the 1839 Paris series in a slightly different form. The previous lithograph had been derived originally, by way of a traced wash drawing (Plate 51), from the watercolour of 1833 (Plate 49). In 1839 Boys again revises the figural composition which he had worked out in 1835. This is seen in a preparatory tracing-paper drawing in the British Museum which has a rather loosely traced architectural background with detailed figures overdrawn in the foreground (Plate 52A). This suggests that Boys, satisfied with the architecture which he had drawn in 1835, was intent on producing a different figure composition. It exhibits a series of ideas, and at the left one can see the group pictured in the 1835 lithograph, now the only remaining feature from that version. Among the successive ideas that he has depicted is a horse and cart; the background figures at the right appear more or less as in the final chromolithograph. This evolutionary process shows that Boys, although relying on earlier prototypes, was more than prepared to experiment to achieve a more felicitous composition (Plate 52).

The major difference between this series of views and the previous ones is that these were chromo-lithographs, a new departure in the history of lithography. Boys was not the first to introduce colours into lithography; Senefelder, the inventor of lithography, had experimented with colour margins in Strixner's *Albrecht Dürers Christlich-Mythologische Hand-zeichnungen,*[4] and Engelmann in France had received a *brevet d'invention* (patent) for a new method of colour printing in 1837. Both men, however, printed colours from the same stone, a method which had its defects, as noted by *The Art Union* in 1831.[5] In England Owen Jones with his *Alhambra,*[6] started in 1836 but not published until 1842, made lithographs printed in colours from several stones to render his architectural decoration. Boys evidently knew of this publication because he referred to it indirectly in his introductory descriptive notice for the Paris series:

> Chromolithography . . . in its application to this class of subjects . . . has been carried so far beyond what was required in copying polychrome architecture, hieroglyphics, arabesques, etc., . . . that it has become almost a new art.

Here Boys brings together the two salient characteristics of his Paris series, their technical invention and their distinction as works of art. As explained above, chromolithography is the reproduction in lithography of colours printed from separate stones. These supplemented an ordinary lithographic drawing which provided the basic framework. Boys used four or five different colours: each colour, printed from a different stone, was printed successively on the paper to produce the final chromolithograph. The overall effect being obtained by, in his own words, 'using the primitive colours for the first tints, and producing variety of tints by their successive super or juxtapositions'.[7]

It is fortunate that the technical method of reproduction used by Boys is described in a letter which he wrote to *The Probe* on 10 January 1840. This was in response to a letter written by Hullmandel (who printed the Paris series) claiming that he was the inventor of the innovations embodied in that series.[8] This exchange of letters was sparked off by a review in *The Probe* which spoke of Boys as 'the inventor of a new power of multiplying coloured landscapes on paper'. This is what Boys wrote:

> The high praise passed on my work by your review of last month, and the kind testimonial of Mr Hullmandel, smooth down any angry feelings which might arise at his surreptitious claims, put forth in his letters addressed to you. With all due respect for, and acknowledgement of his great many claims on the reconnaisance of artists, still, I cannot tamely submit to have it given out that I am indebted to him for this invention. I am, Sir, *entirely* the originator and *inventor* of my work, as set before the public; within myself the idea originated, of producing a wash by lithography printed in colour, using the primitive colours for the first tints, and producing variety of tints by their successive super or juxtapositions. But I think I perceive the drift of Mr Hullmandel's letter;

it is no more than to claim for himself the invention, and put forth the advantages of stumping.

This, as he shows, however, has been used by Harding, Lewis, Nash, etc. for many years.[9] I allow the great capabilities of 'stumping' in *certain* cases where the artist can use it; but I must here state that my ways are not his ways; the means by which I have produced my tints, are my own. *Chromolithography is totally independent of 'stumping', if the artist pleases, and in most instances is better in its absence.*

I claim not for myself to have been the first to make use of this new power; though I am conscious of no antecedent, yet I cannot, I will not, allow to Mr Hullmandel the liberty of statement that 'I only adopted the invention of which he claims the merit, by furnishing me with a new and desirable material'. I deny it. If he refers to stumping, where is the novelty of a material used by Harding in his 'Sketches at Home and Abroad'? or by Lewis?[10] Besides we see by this, that it is no necessary concomitant of colour, otherwise we should have works antecedent to mine. I have, from my first insight to the powers of lithography, desired to produce colour. My first offer to put it into practice was to produce a facsimile of Stanfield's drawing of the moonlight, in his work.[11] The publisher, Mr Hodgson, can bear testimony to this; but I was given to understand, by Mr Hullmandel that it was impracticable; then it was I determined to do something of my own: my Picturesque Architecture was commenced, and progressed towards the perfecting of the art.

Now allow me to say a word or two on the means by which I have produced my tints, in contradistinction with Mr Hullmandel's method. I produce a variety of tints in the skies, and the masses of light, by what is termed by aquatint engravers, brush-biting, that is, laying on to the ground work of chalk or ink, weak acid, and with a camel's hair pencil, where I want light, thus *positively painting with the brush,* and scraping in the forms of the whites. I produce the full tints with *lithographic ink* laid with a brush on the parts required; and the half-tints by rubbing down the aforesaid ink with a piece of cloth to the tint required, and then strengthening it again with ink in its forcible parts. I even modulate the strength of my ink, by which I can produce a variety of tints, though I was informed that ink was ink. It is by this means that I have produced the variations in the lights, the washes, and that closeness of texture in the solid surfaces referred to: but be it not supposed that I do not use the stump, but it is as an artist ever does: using the first thing that comes to hand that is in any way adapted to produce the desired end. Now in just praise, and as due to Mr Hullmandel, let me add, that it is to his care and keeping we must confide ourselves after all our labours, and in safer hands we cannot place ourselves; his knowledge of his art is as consummate as his love of art: and I am sure he will not quarrel with me for thus desiring to maintain the principle of 'cui cuique refertur' of our school days.

With very many apologies for the length of this letter,
I remain, Dear Sir,
Your most obedient servant,
Thomas Shotter Boys.

It is a fascinating letter and reveals much about the exact method by which Boys produced his chromolithographs. Hullmandel, in his letter, had referred to the 'modesty of this talented artist', and it is clear that Boys was reluctant to commit his feelings to paper, but felt that he could not tamely submit to 'Hullmandel's surreptitious claims'. He was obviously proud of his own inventiveness in this field. In the letter he does not claim to have invented the stumping method, which, as he said, was by 1839 no innovation in any case. He admits that the principle of colour printing in lithography had been conceived of before (by Senefelder, as Hullmandel was quick to point out in a subsequent letter),[12] though, as has been stated above, his chromolithography was different from the early colour printing lithography.

In effect Boys was right to claim that he was the originator and inventor of his own work, he even says that he had suggested it for an earlier publication but that Hullmandel, despite his 'knowledge of his art', had been discouraging about the possibility. Boys proceeded to follow his own path by himself 'using the first thing that comes to hand that is in any way adapted to produce the desired end', obviously revelling in experimentation. After the drawing was made it was to Hullmandel that Boys entrusted his work, the former printed the plates and ensured that they were faithful in both idea and practice to Boys's original. In his reply Hullmandel limited himself to claiming that he had invented stumping (a fact which Boys never denied) and to saying that Boys had used the 'means and materials' supplied by himself. He never disputes that the conception and development of chromolithography, as displayed in the Paris series, was anything but Boys's own.

Boys had previously mastered the properties of this new medium, incorporating as it did all the most recent inventions such as lithotint, stumping, brush-biting, modulation of the strength of inks and rubbing with a piece of cloth. He exhibits complete confidence in the manner in which he attempts to create different effects in his chromolithographs; his aim was to approximate to differing types of watercolour drawings and oil paintings. In his descriptive notice he writes that:

> The view of the *Abbaye of St Armand, Rouen,* is intended to present the appearance of a crayon sketch heightened with colour: that of the *Ste-Chapelle, Paris,* a sepia drawing, with touches of colour: the *Fish Market, Antwerp,* a slight sketch in watercolours; *St Laurent,* a finished watercolour drawing . . .

And so on. This exhibition of facility and versatility would have appealed to prospective buyers, who viewed the series as imitating other artistic mediums.[13] As such they represented the culmination of the whole trend of lithography during the 1830s, that is, towards the imitation of watercolour drawings.

Technical mastery apart, these chromolithographs (Plates 56–60) are brilliant works of art. The composition of each was carefully devised and the delicate disposition of colours and tones reflects the best qualities of Boys's watercolour style. The colours are marvellously bright and resonant, giving a clear and sparkling quality to the lithographs. They represent Boys's definitive views of Paris, the result of a decade of depicting its streets and character, and they display a total involvement which was born out of love for the subject tempered by a rare gift for observation.

He called the series *Picturesque Architecture* and they truly present views of picturesque buildings, but preserve the contemporary character and life of the streets. He carefully records the signs on the shops, the price-tags of goods for sale, the overhead street-lamps, the modern, old and the more obscure unromanticized quarters of Paris. Despite his ideal of accuracy, he did not hesitate to change the appearance of the scene for the sake of his impression. The changes made produced a better pictorial composition, but they were also depicting Paris truer to herself than she really was by preserving the essence of what he saw concentrated into the small space of his picture. He relives for us today the Paris of the 1830s, recording its lost appearances and character.

The financial burden of producing the Paris series must have been considerable. Possibly Thomas Boys, the printer, was responsible for much of its financing. *The Art Union* recorded that 'we can scarcely imagine the labour and expense will be sufficiently recompensed'.[14] A large advertising programme was organized to sell the series. Boys pulled a number of trial proofs, called specimens, which were sent round, together with a prospectus, to the papers and art journals of the day. *The Probe* review refers with disgust to 'the meretricious puffery of prospectus advertising',[15] which was considered in bad taste in that period. The prospectus talks of Boys's reputation (albeit little known) and his achievements as a lithographic draughtsman, and stated that:

> This work will correspond, in size with those of Roberts and Stanfield, but it will be bound in a very elegant and superior style, fit for the drawing room table.

No expense was spared in producing a 'coffee-table book' for the enjoyment of the art connoisseurs and the aristocracy of England.[16] Despite the solicitation of such advertisements the merits of the book were proclaimed by reviewers, and for the most part it was well received—

48

though there were some adverse comments.[17] In a review of his *London as it is* a correspondent wrote in 1842 that:

> Mr Boys has already secured a favourable reception with the public; the merits of his illustrations of 'France' etc. have been universally acknowledged.[18]

Whether the publication ever made enough money to pay for its production will never be known.

Boys did not go bankrupt and felt sufficiently encouraged to produce a sequel—*London as it is*—less than three years later. He must have started on this very soon after the Paris series was printed as he had to begin from scratch and make original drawings and sketches from which he could derive the lithographs, a process involving a considerable length of time. But, before the London project, he also completed *A series of views in York,* published in 1841 by R. Sunter in York.[19] Despite his disagreements with Hullmandel, it was the latter who printed these lithographs. As a project it was altogether less ambitious than the Paris and London series, comprising ten lithographs with one beige tint. Small in scale and published locally, it could not have been seen as a major series and would hardly have increased Boys's reputation, and it is surprising that he ever took it on—except as a money-making commission. It seems that he had started on this series at an early stage as one of the plates is signed and dated 1837.[20] The lithographs have a certain quality in their drawing and portrayal of local character, but they represent a lowering in standards compared to the Paris series.

London as it is was obviously seen as complementary in theme and scale to the Paris series. Unlike the Paris views, it was not published in chromolithography, possibly for financial reasons. However, the London series represents a new development in lithography. The trend in the 1830s had been towards eliminating the qualities of lithography which distinguished it from watercolour pictures. Thus Hullmandel spoke with admiration about the stump's capability of obtaining 'substance and depth of tint . . . without the sandy, open, granulated texture of ordinary lithography'.[21] Boys's Paris series represents the high water-mark of this ambition. In the London series it is the qualities of lithography rather than watercolour that are uppermost. He presents lithography as an art form in its own right.

There are no known watercolours which correspond directly to any of the lithographs in the London series. There are several watercolours of *London from Greenwich Hill* (e.g. Plate 34) but they are all different from the view in the lithograph.[22] The conclusion one comes to is that Boys never made any watercolours for the London series. By this time he had developed a sophisticated process in the creation of his lithographs which involved tracing-paper drawings. It appears that Boys made these drawings on the spot during 1840. In a private collection in America there are pencil on tracing-paper drawings for *Blackfriars from Southwark Bridge* inscribed *sketched 22.4.1840,* and for the *Doorway, Temple church* inscribed *sketched 8.4.1840.*[23] These drawings made on the spot (possibly with a Graphic Telescope) provide the raw material for the lithographs; from these Boys improvised his compositions and figures in further orange chalk and pencil tracing drawings in the same collection. Sketches which might have provided him with his tone values have not come to light. In the Paris series the tones and colours had been built up on the drawing and colour stones in imitation of his original watercolours, which served as guides. The London series represents a further diversification of his method. He drew the outline on the spot, added improvisations by means of tracing-paper drawings and then transferred the whole on to the lithographic stone without any tones or shading, just like a line drawing. On a second stone he washed in the tones and masses of the composition, without any drawing. This was a simplification and ultimately a purification of technique. Essentially, the first was a pencil drawing, the second was a wash sketch, the two being combined to produce the finished lithograph.

The Guildhall Library in London possesses a book of proofs for the London series. This comprises an 'outline proof', a 'tint proof', and a final proof for each view. Those for *The Strand* (Plates 63–65) display this process well. The outline proof (Plate 63), developed from a tracing drawing is clear and precise, the touch is firm and confident. The shading and hatching describe the texture and appearance of the architecture by line alone, the sky is left completely bare. The tint proof (Plate 64) is, however, purely a tonal sketch in lithotint with no attempt to portray texture. Sketched with a brush, the masses of buildings, crowds and clouds are painted in, but there is no descriptive detail in the architecture or the figures. In the final printing, the outline and the tint come together to create a feeling of space and solidity such as would be inconceivable in a simple one-stone lithograph drawing. The effect is so harmonious as to appear almost indivisible, but Boys was able to visualize the two elements both apart and together, and then combine them without one dominating the other. The finishing touches were added when the lithographs were hand-coloured subsequent to their printing (Plate 65).

Boys conceived of the colouring as distinct from the drawing and tinting. In his watercolours the skilful use of colour as both tone and texture (as well as colour) was one of their outstanding features, but here the colour is universally thin and transparent. The tonal and textural qualities of the views are rendered by the lithography rather than by the colours, thus the use of colouring here is the reverse of that in his watercolour technique. Tradition has it that Boys himself coloured some of the London series;[24] certainly it must be true that, even if he did not carry out the colouring himself, he directed it, for the colours are so tasteful and do in fact enhance the qualities of the lithography (Plates 65–71).

This colouring was an embellishment: originally Boys had conceived of the lithographs as uncoloured apart from the sepia colouring of the tint stone. Copies which might have been coloured by Boys or his helpers are rare (though many were coloured by other artists at a later date).[25] The colouring gives the effect of a watercolour drawing; but this effect differs from Boys's own watercolours, to which the Paris series had attempted to approximate. The best hand-coloured lithographs are so exquisite that it seems impossible that Boys had ever intended that they should be colourless. He obviously wanted to present them as monochrome prints exhibiting the pure qualities of lithography as against other mediums. It was probably the commercial enterprise of his cousin, the publisher, that persuaded him to offer coloured versions for sale together with the uncoloured sepia ones. As monochrome lithographs the technical mastery of the London series is unsurpassed, and as hand-coloured lithographs they are among the most attractive works of art produced in the nineteenth century. Today, much of their attraction and interest lies in the depiction of a London that is lost forever. It is strange that few other artists produced series on London in early Victorian days. As some of the critics of the day pointed out, English artists, dictated to by the tastes of their buying public, tended to concentrate their search for the picturesque on the Continent:

> During a quarter of a century, the street scenery chiefly painted by our artists, recommended itself on account of some 'picturesque' feature; and when this was wanting, it was supplied by means of a little ragged mannerism.[26] At home we have but little to meet this taste, which has been fostered principally by matter from the continent . . . works like this under notice were not thought of: continuous straight lines and plain facades were uninteresting, and extremely difficult of treatment; hence that with which the artist has here had to contend is, first, the substantial difficulties of his subjects and afterwards the caprice of conventional taste.[27]

Boys concentrated on the well known scenes of London life, and the streets whose architecture must have been overfamiliar to its inhabitants. Depicting these scenes necessitated precision in

XVIII

XIX

FIGURE XVIII **THE PORCH AT RATISBON CATHEDRAL,** by Samuel Prout (1783–1852).
Watercolour, $25\frac{3}{4} \times 18\frac{1}{4}$ ins/654 × 463 mm.
Victoria and Albert Museum, London (1040–1873).
Reproduced by courtesy of the Victoria and Albert Museum.

FIGURE XIX **A GOTHIC ARCHWAY,** by Samuel Prout (1783–1852).
Watercolour, $13\frac{1}{2} \times 9\frac{1}{2}$ ins/343 × 241 mm.
Signed (Monogram on wall) SP
Private Collection, England.

detail, hence Boys's aim was to portray 'London as it is'. A feature of the views is the way in which he manages to combine accuracy with artistic qualities. He was not afraid of picturing the swarming bustle of the city crowds, street repair workmen, removal men or beggars as the subjects of his foregrounds. For historians, Boys's social accuracy is of great importance as it documented everyday life. The camera had not yet been invented, so Boys's lithographs are unique as social documents. He also depicts London landmarks which have now disappeared: The Temple Bar, the Board of Trade in Whitehall and the Egyptian Hall in Piccadilly.

Although we think that our way of life today is very different from that of the early Victorians, some of the remarks made in the reviews of *London as it is* reveal preoccupation with problems still pertinent today:

> In the picture as in the reality this part of London as it is [The Strand] seems almost impassable for foot passengers, and somewhat dangerous for those in carriages . . . How precious land is for building and with what difficulty the pressure of population is restrained from the occupancy of every untenanted spot in the metropolis.[28]

NOTES TO CHAPTER FOUR

1 Letter of 1833 cited, and quoted below.
2 *Ibid.* In this letter Boys is referring, among others, to the following publications: Thomas Girtin's *A Selection of Twenty of the most Picturesque views in Paris*, London, 1803: *Picturesque Views of the City of Paris and its environs*, by Frederick Nash (1782–1856), London, 1823; *Views of Paris and Environs*, by Augustus Charles Pugin (1762–1832), London, 1828–32, and *Twelve of the most remarkable Views in Paris and the Environs*, by Israel Silvestre (1621–91). These references testify to the fact that Boys made detailed studies of the engraved works of other artists, both contemporary and of other periods.
3 British Museum, London (1952.5.10.9.35) and in a private collection in America.
4 Published in Munich in 1808. It is unlikely that Boys was familiar with this book.
5 'Colour lithography is more laborious and ingenious than useful, and neither in cheapness nor effect does it equal the print coloured by hand in the ordinary way. It cannot allow of graduation of colours or blending of tints; and the most it is capable of, seems to be the representation of Mosaic or printed glass windows.' *The Art Union*, 1831, page 201.
6 Published in London in 1842.
7 *The Probe*, February 1840, page 278.
8 Hullmandel's first letter, written on 5 December 1839, appeared on page 262. Boys's appeared in February 1840, page 278.
9 Harding, *op. cit.*; Joseph Nash, *Architecture of the Middle Ages*, London, 1838.
10 John Frederick Lewis, *Sketches of Spain and Spanish Character*, London, 1836.
11 Stanfield, *op. cit.*, Plate XV.
12 Written on 14 February 1840, it appeared on page 13 of the 1 April edition of *The Probe*. Hullmandel also enclosed 'supporting' letters from Harding and Nash. All these letters dwelt at length on stumping, and did not refute Boys's claim to have invented chromolithography.
13 *The Quarterly Review.*
14 *The Art Union*, October 1839, page 139.
15 *The Probe*, 15 August 1839, pages 172–173.
16 Boys printed his Descriptive Notice and Commentary in both English and French, hoping to find a market in France.
17 For example, *The Probe*, article cited.
18 Anonymous review preserved in the Guildhall Library, London.
19 Groschwitz, *op. cit.*, Check List No. 30.
20 Plate I, *St Helen's Square and Stonegate*.
21 *The Probe*, letter cited.
22 Plate VI.
23 Respectively Plate VII and the Frontispiece.
24 *Original Views of London as it is, by Thomas Shotter Boys, 1842*, by E.B. Chancellor, London, 1926; page 4: 'It is said that thirty were actually tinted by Boys himself.'
25 See Note 24. Forgeries are common. The British Museum, London possesses a folder of examples, with an explanatory note by J.L. Douthwaite.
26 The writer is referring here to such artists as Samuel Prout (see Figures XVIII and XIX).
27 *The Art Union*, 1842, page 33.
28 Undated extract from a supplement to *The Times* of 1842, preserved in the Guildhall Library, London.

V
LAST YEARS

THE widely acclaimed success of Boys's Paris and London series achieved for him a position of some eminence as an artist. In 1840 he had been elected the first associate of the New Water-colour Society, an accomplishment of distinction for an artist who had not been resident in England for most of his working career. In 1841 he was elected a full member. When he returned to England in 1837 he had taken up residence in Albany Street. Presumably his finances were not such that he was able to buy a house, since in the period that followed he moved through a succession of different addresses.[1] It is likely that the two lithographic series, although artistically a success, did not produce any great financial reward—as the reviewer in *The Art Union* had foreseen. However, they did bring him royal patronage. King Louis-Philippe of France had been presented, through Callow,[2] with a copy of the Paris series. Boys had in turn received a flattering letter and a ring, but not before they had been sent in error to Thomas Boys the publisher. The ring formed a brooch, with the initials L.P. and the French crown in diamonds.[3] For the London series he received a letter and a watch. It is possible that Boys's work came to the notice of Queen Victoria at about this time as, in 1843, she gave a Shotter Boys watercolour as a wedding present to Princess Clémentine, the daughter of Louis-Philippe.[4]

Once he had achieved his high reputation, Boys's problem was to find a way of keeping it. During the early 1840s he exhibited works at the New Water-colour Society, though not in great numbers. His only exhibit in 1842 was a *Coastal Scene,* which received the following review:

> A pretty little bit, but by no means sufficient to uphold the reputation of an artist, who has a reputation which he ought not to risk. This is merely an excuse for keeping his name on the exhibition list.[5]

To maintain his standing it was necessary for him to produce either a series of major watercolours or a new lithographic work.

It is possible that he went abroad in 1842 with that very idea in mind. His sister Mary and her husband, William John Cooke, had left England to live in Darmstadt in the spring of 1840. W. J. Cooke's cousin, Edward William, was soon to go and visit them in July of that year.[6] As Boys was more closely related, it is not surprising to find that he himself visited them between the summers of 1842 and 1843. In 1843 at the New Water-colour Society exhibition he showed views of Antwerp, Prague, Wartburg, Dresden and Eisenach.[7] Darmstadt would have been a convenient base from which to make sketching tours in Germany. From this time onwards his views of Germany appeared intermittently at the New Water-colour Society exhibitions. Tracing-paper drawings do exist of German series, though they are mostly undated.[8] It appears that Boys did not make sketch books while on these tours and many of the tracing-paper drawings have perished. However, it is difficult to see how he could have executed watercolours of German subjects after his return to England without the aid of some sort of sketches or notes.

During the rest of Boys's life his watercolours exhibit a wide range of styles which suggest that he was searching for a definitive style which would bring him artistic success and financial reward. He tried many devices to create security for himself and his wife, Célestine.[9] As he grew older his travelling to the Continent must have gradually petered out, but he was made a member of the Société Libre des Beaux Arts[10] and of the Société Aquarelliste des Belges[11] which indicates that he must have spent some time abroad during this period, particularly as the Belgian society was not formed until 1856.

In 1842, before he went on his trip to Germany to visit his sister and brother-in-law, he must have made a tour through the Midlands to Shrewsbury as there is a view of *The Racecourse at Shrewsbury taken from the Grandstand* (Plate 72). This watercolour shows a marked departure from his style of the 1830s: it is a loose and sketchy work making no attempt to recapture the precision of technique that had been his earlier hallmark. It is purely a landscape, and as such naturally would not necessitate the exact treatment required by an architectural subject. The careful and dry treatment of his *View of Greenwich* of 1830 (Plate 34) is left behind in this drawing, with its fluid massing of forms by broad washes of wet colour (a *View of the Edge of a Heath* approximates very closely to this work and must have been done on the same sketching tour).[12] One reason for comparing these later watercolours to the Greenwich views is that the character of Boys's work changed with each shift in location between England and France. As the Greenwich views (Plates 33 and 34) had displayed a different feeling to his French work of the 1830s, so these views show a similar degree of divergence; the air is clearer and fresher, there is a sparkle and clarity which contrast with the diffused air of his Paris watercolours (*e.g.* Plate 16).

Clearly, his return to England had produced a change in style; it also seems to have engendered a change in outlook. In this later period it was perhaps Boys's willingness to react differently according to the scenes in front of him that dictated this new approach, while at the same time he was searching for a successful and individual style. The sketchy mood of the Shrewsbury view is continued in 1844 in a small sepia sketch of *St Paul's from Lambeth* (Plate 73) in which a strong sky is rendered with purposefully messy brushwork. He cleverly picks out the forms of the boats, dark against the sky and water, and of St Paul's which appears light against the menacing clouds. The Thames is rendered in dragged washes of dry colour drawn horizontally across the paper, a characteristic which is always found in Boys's watercolours. In this same year he must have paid a visit to the Channel Islands; a view of a *Tower near St Helier, Jersey*[13] gives the impression of a brief sketch made on the spot, and the colours are restrained but fresh.

These watercolours were all *plein-air* sketches made in front of the object and were not for exhibition. There also exists an interesting series of watercolours of Durham from this period. In 1845 at the New Water-colour Society Boys exhibited a *View of Durham* (probably Plate 75). There is also a sketch (Plate 74), presumably preparatory, which has the same fluidity of treatment as the watercolours mentioned above. The sky is washed in with thick bars of wet paint—though the composition is more architectonic than the Thames sketch (Plate 73). Boys has scratched out with a knife white lines across the water: this feature also appears in the large watercolour of the cathedral (Plate 75) which is very carefully and drily treated; there is none of the freedom of his sketch, and the granulation of washes and the over-working with the knife and brush hark back to his earlier style. The cathedral lacks the detailed and precise architectural brushwork of such paintings as the *Notre Dame, Paris* (Plate 20). This overall dry treatment recalls in particular the view of *The Castle Mills and Bridge over the Foss at York* (Plate 38) of ten years earlier. The foreground figures in both watercolours are strikingly similar in style and idiom. The Durham view is more mature in treatment and less diffuse than the York view, but the two show a startling consistency in modes of representation over a period of ten years.

By 1846[14] Boys's financial position was such that he resorted to trying his hand at being a drawing master (in Cheltenham). This was a popular pursuit of artists who regarded it as a potboiling business: Cox, Callow, Harding, Prout and Cotman were among those famous artists who took to teaching. For Boys it was never meant to be a permanent arrangement as he kept on his lodgings at 81 Great Titchfield Street in London. On 30 October he wrote a letter to his friend Henry Mogford from his temporary abode at 10 Rodney Terrace, Cheltenham:

> Here we are after a week's sojourn and very comfortably lodged and pleased with the place with the exception that I am afraid I shall not succeed. I find there are *six* other drawing masters and I am advertising and leaving about cards at the libraries & spas etc. etc. I never did the dirty so before. I find all the masters do it here . . . Mrs Dale . . . is a nice plump soul, my god Mogford I have been so knocked about in the world that you do not know how kind I felt her conduct . . . Penley[15] says he teaches as ever that he has never given up, but tells me not to count on the place at all, that if it was not for portraits he could not do. So I shall I fear be floored. I shall work away for the London exhibitions en attendant [Plate 79]. I hope in my next I may be able to give you better news.[16]

A thoroughly depressing letter. Obviously Boys has been in bad straits when he complains that he has been 'knocked about in the world'. The attempt to become a drawing master looks rather like an act of desperation, which even Boys thought was doomed to failure from the start. It is not surprising that, in such a pessimistic frame of mind, he could not produce works of great artistry which would uphold his flagging reputation. His ambition and will to succeed of earlier years had clearly gone. He was still proud enough to feel that it was debasing for an artist with an international reputation to have to solicit custom amongst the idle rich at the spas.

His watercolours of the next few years lack any real identity of their own. He resorted to reworking the themes of his earlier successes. In the 1849 New Water-colour Society Exhibition he showed another version of the *Old Hôtel de Ville St Omer,* which had been destroyed in 1831.[17] Also in that year he exhibited *Amiens, seen from the banks of the Somme* (Plate 83), mammoth in proportions, impressive in composition, but lacking in feeling and delicacy of touch, and obviously an attempt to recapture the style of his earlier years. This major work in Boys's *oeuvre,*[18] which followed the current trend of attempting to rival oil paintings (*e.g.* Figures XX and XXI) in size, treatment and complexity of composition was received well by a reviewer in *The Art Journal*:

> The composition is judiciously enlivened by river craft and figures, and forced into powerful effect by opposition of tone.[19]

As ever his mastery of tone lifted him out of mediocrity, but the colouring is confined to murky greens, browns and yellowy tints. It is impressive but not exhilarating.

Strangely, Boys did not carry out much engraving work during the 1840s. He lithographed two watercolours for publications by Catherwood and Lieutenant-Colonel Jack which were of no great distinction.[20] His *Architecture Pittoresque dessinée d'après Nature* of 1835 was re-issued in Paris by Turgis.[21] His one original work of the 1840s in lithography was the production of two lithotints of Picardy for Volume III, Part 2 of Baron Taylor's *Voyages Pittoresques*.[22] In *La Tour de Beffroi, Calais* (Plate 76) he has sketched everything with a brush; there is no drawing as such. The effect is light and airy, and marks a feat of brilliant brushwork. The tones are slight and loose—a contrast to the character of his earlier lithographs.

At the beginning of the 1850s he was employed by John Ruskin to etch and lithograph a number of illustrations for his *Examples of the Architecture of Venice*[23] and the *Stones of Venice*.[24] Thomas Lupton filled in Boys's etched outlines with mezzotint. The British Museum possesses an etched outline of an *Architectural subject with door head* (Plate 84) similar in format to but not included in the *Examples of the Architecture of Venice*. The lines are exceptionally fine, conveying detail and atmosphere with ease and facility. Ruskin recognized the quality of Boys's work:

XX

XXI

FIGURE XX **LEANING TOWER AT BOLOGNA,** by William Callow (1812–1908).
Watercolour, $16\frac{3}{10} \times 12\frac{9}{10}$ ins/415 × 327 mm.
Signed (BR) <u>Wm Callow/1864</u>
Victoria and Albert Museum, London (F.52).
Reproduced by courtesy of the Victoria and Albert Museum.

FIGURE XXI **L'HOTEL DE VILLE, LEIPZIG,** by William Callow (1812–1908).
Watercolour, $28\frac{15}{16} \times 23\frac{13}{16}$ ins/735 × 579 mm.
Signed (BL) <u>William Callow/1854</u>
Fondation Custodia, Institut Néerlandais, Paris (1970.7.21).

56

Copies from my pen drawings etched by Mr Boys with a fidelity for which I sincerely thank him.[25]

He was paid £30.10s. for each plate that he etched; a not inconsiderable sum in Victorian days for 'hack' engraving work. Unfortunately Ruskin never praised Boys in any of his writings, preferring to give his lavish and influential admiration to other, lesser artists.

Boys hoped to continue in the field of reproducing purely architectural work when he advertised his services in *The Builder* of 1851:

TO ARCHITECTS

COMPETITION and other DRAWINGS,—

Mr THOMAS S. BOYS, member of the New Society of Painters in Water Colours, and author of 'The Picturesque Architecture of Paris, Ghent, Rouen, &c.', and of 'London as it is', offers his services in Tinting Backgrounds, Landscapes, Perspective Views, Interiors, &c. From the long experience he has had in such subjects, he is fully aware of the points necessary to be attended to Drawings and designs lithographed in a superior manner.—
Address, Mr BOYS, 24 Albany-street, Regent's-park.[26]

A series of watercolours portraying Cowley Manor in Gloucestershire (purchased at the artist's sale at 30 Acacia Road) represents the type of work that Boys was employed on as the result of this advertisement.[27] Cowley Manor was acquired by James Hutchinson in about 1852 and soon after he employed George Somers Clarke, the architect, to remodel the existing seventeenth-century building and its gardens. This work was completed by the late 1850s. Boys's watercolour drawings (before they were cut up) must have formed a panorama of the whole facade of the building (Plate 90). The pencil detail is very precise and almost mechanical, characteristics that might be expected in a drawing for an architect. But these watercolours are much more than simple architectural drawings: they are pictorial realizations of technical plans.

Clarke may in fact have employed Boys to make what are now called artistic designs from his bare architectural drawings so that Hutchinson could see what the proposed remodelling was going to look like before he gave the final go-ahead. The figures are sketched on as supplements to the basic architectural colouring to add life and atmosphere. The complete and unremitting attention to detail is almost unreal, and certainly is uncharacteristic of Boys's watercolours of comparative date (Plate 82). Their function apart, they are also beautiful works of art; the figures washed in with bright and vivid colours, the sky fresh and alive, the trees sketched with quick and imaginative strokes of the brush. Their double identity as architectural drawings and delicate works of art lends them a unique attraction.

Ambrose Poynter, whom Boys had instructed in watercolours when they were both in Paris, had become an architect of some distinction. He was a founder member of the Royal Institute of British Architects. He had designed and built many buildings and was still a practising architect.[28] In 1852 his son, Edward Poynter, later to become President of the Royal Academy, was taught the art of watercolour painting by Boys. This service was probably done as a favour to his old friend Poynter, who wanted his son to receive the same teaching as he himself had benefited from at an earlier date. It is unlikely that Ambrose Poynter was able to aid Boys in his desire to make drawings for architects, though he may have furnished him with some introductions.

In 1852 Boys was commissioned to make watercolour drawings for a work on *Apsley House and Walmer Castle* (Plates 88 and 89), the homes of the Duke of Wellington. The colour lithographs (partly hand-coloured) were made from Boys's drawings by employees of the Hanharts, who were well-known lithographic printers. The light and vibrant qualities of the watercolours (Plate 87) are lost in the lithographs where the colours are vulgar reds, yellows and blues. They could hardly have done Boys's reputation any good and are a disaster by any standards. As well as painting watercolours, Boys here continued his practice of making orange chalk and pencil tracing-paper drawings.[29] These are sketchy in character and must have been drawn on the spot. They have colour directions pencilled on to them, and presumably it was from these that he made the finished watercolours from which the lithographers could work.

A sketch of *Walmer Castle looking East towards Deal* (Plate 86) continues his vivid sketching style in relatively small-scale works. It was made by Boys as a study in its own right, and captures vividly the contrasts of colour and warmth in the sky with bold sweeps of the brush. In the same informal vein there is a sepia *Sketch of a Street scene,*[30] which relates stylistically to the *Lodge in a Park* of the Cowley series. The washes are not so controlled, but the feel is similar and the method of daubing wet paint to form the masses of the trees follows on closely from the treatment in the Cowley picture. Briefly done, it has depth and light achieved by the clever disposition of the tones and textures of the sepia. It is not as loose as the earlier 1840s sketches, which displayed a less strict control over the handling of the washes which often overlapped in a seemingly haphazard manner. The overall tonal harmony is carefully regulated, taking account of the relative dryness, wetness and opacity of each wash; it is a slight work, but a little masterpiece of mood and expression.

In 1853 or early 1854 Boys must have revisited Jersey since seven of his watercolours exhibited during 1854 were of this island. He sent three of these to the New Water-colour Society, and another four in December 1854 to the Amateur Artists' Gallery at 121 Pall Mall, of which institution Henry Mogford was the secretary. With these Boys wrote an accompanying letter, on 29 November, from his lodgings at 32 Albany Street:

> I send for your Winter Exhibition four small drawings which I hope to God you may sell as it would be a true Godsend to oblige an old friend by doing your possible.
>
> They are: £
> Havre du Port Jersey   15.15.0d.
> Tour de Rozel, from Boulay Bay, Jersey   14.14.0d.
> St Aubin's Bay, Jersey   12.12.0d.
> Elizabeth Castle, Jersey   7. 7.0d.[31]

Obviously Boys was still in severe financial difficulties, yet these prices could hardly have provided more than temporary help. At the New Water-colour Society *Havre du Port, Jersey* had been offered at £12.5.0d. and *Elizabeth Castle* at £6.16.0d. It seems odd that if they had been unsold, he should have put up the price at the subsequent exhibition. A possibility is that they had already been sold and these were second versions, and that he was hoping to cash in on a successful subject—a practice which he had favoured in the 1830s. This interpretation is supported by the fact that two years later, in 1856, he exhibited at the New Water-colour Society four watercolours, two of *London from Southwark Bridge* and two of *St Aubin's Bay, Jersey.* The first two were on offer at £28.15.0d. and £28.15.6d., the latter pair both at £13.13.6d., one being distinguished from the other in the catalogue as hanging on the first screen.[32]

The continuing decline in the fortunes of the Boys family took a further knock, when in 1859 Thomas Boys, the publisher who had earlier provided so much valuable support for Shotter Boys, had to retire from publishing because of an unsuccessful business venture.[33] Unfortunately it was at this very same time that Shotter Boys might have conceived of a new series to follow up his earlier lithographed works. In 1858 and 1859 he made extensive tours through Wales and the Midlands,[34] and his exhibits at the New Water-colour Society for 1859 and 1860 are almost exclusively of views in these areas.[35] He intended to call this series *Remains of Old England,* and it was to be based on townscape views of old and picturesque parts of ancient cities such as Salisbury, Shrewsbury, Tewkesbury and Worcester. The views are all quite large and detailed in treatment (Plates 92 and 93). They show life in provincial England: the deserted sunbathed streets of a picturesque quarter in Shrewsbury, the open stalls and shops, the farmer bringing in his cow to market, cuts of meat hanging in butchers' windows and other such characteristic episodes in the daily life of these market towns. The architecture is rather exaggerated with its picturesque sloping roofs and beams bent by the strain of age. The treatment lacks the crisp precision of his earlier days, but the overall appearance is rather splendid. No lithographic series of these views was ever produced, perhaps because of his own financial difficulties and the demise of his cousin who could no longer sponsor or publish it. The idea was soon discarded since none of Boys's watercolours after this date bears the additional title of *Remains of Old England*.

This fresh attempt at producing a series of works shows that Boys still had energy and ambitions left which could inspire him to further efforts. The views of Wales with which he also concerned himself at this time provided a new departure in his watercolours. Unfortunately very few are known. The Victoria and Albert Museum possesses a view inscribed on the reverse: *The Vale of Llangollen* (Plate 94). Possibly this was the work entitled *Vale of Llangollen, North Wales* that was exhibited at the New Water-colour Society in 1862, for sale at £11. More likely it may be a preparatory sketch since it has the appearance of a slight wash dashed off on the spot without any later studio alterations. Furthermore, the *Old Row in Watergate Street, Chester* (Plate 96) was on offer at the same exhibition at 5 guineas, and the Victoria and Albert sketch does not seem to merit a price of £11 if the Chester view was available for only 5 guineas. The former is painted in vividly free greens and yellows over a few brief pencil outlines. Fresh and without mannerisms, it might have been painted yesterday. It continues the idiom of his previous sketching style of the 1840s and '50s, but with even more control over the application of the washes.

The Old Row in Watergate Street is a most unusual view of that famous landmark in Chester. The contrast of light and dark is masterly, and the touches of bright bodycolour give accent to the beige tones of the masonry and medieval beams. The concern with the everyday life of people is evidently still of great interest to Boys. Humour is provided by the marvellously expressive row of socks hanging down from one of the beams, almost mocking a sign above them proclaiming *T. S. BOYS PAINTER*.

At that same period, 1861–62, Boys was employed to make perspective drawings for the International Exhibition buildings at South Kensington.[36] The style is consistent with that displayed in the Cowley series of a decade earlier (Plates 90 and 91): the architecture is similarly precise and the figures touched in over the underlying architectural framework are improvised. The function of the drawings was probably that of a pictorial realization of the architect's plans.

Throughout these years his large exhibition views of German towns were appearing annually at the New Water-colour Society.[37] Large detailed pictures (Plates 98 and 99), in imitation of oil paintings, they appear artificially picturesque, far removed from the reality portrayed in the Chester view. They show a technical proficiency and capacity for composition which give them an impressive air despite their rather tired handling. It is unlikely that Boys went back to Germany at this late date,[38] so the probability that they were painted in a studio in England some years after the artist had himself stood in front of the views may account for the mannerism and lack of life which they exhibit. These four types of picture—the lively sketch, the masterly and expressive work, the pictorial realization of architecture, and the more ponderous, large-scale view—testify to the diversity of styles of which Boys was capable at any one period.

During the 1860s Boys, though now verging on old age, continued to exhibit at the New Water-colour Society; between 1860 and his death in 1874 he showed over seventy water-colours.[39] Their subject matter was varied, including views in Czechoslovakia, France, Belgium, Ireland, Jersey and all over England. Watercolours also exist of *The Glacier at Bondhuis, Hardanger Fjord, Norway* (1860)[40] and a view of *Lac Nemi*. The latter was exhibited in 1862. Whether he visited any of these places at this late stage is doubtful, and it is probable that at least some of these are derived from sketches by other artists.[41] He reworked the familiar subjects of his youth— Abbeville, Amiens, Paris, St Omer, Rouen and Caen.

All these familiar scenes were painted afresh; he did not simply exhibit watercolours made forty years earlier. It seems that Boys ran a studio at this period, with assistants and pupils to help him execute commissions and architectural work. Samuel Wilkes, who exhibited at the Royal Academy,[42] was certainly a pupil for a time. In a collection of lithographs and proofs bought at Boys's artist's sale there are many initialled *S.W.*[43] Boys probably taught his pupils lithography and he apparently still possessed some of the old lithographic stones of his earlier days, as there are some impressions pulled on china paper of his 1845 lithotints for the *Voyages Pittoresques*. There are also many unfamiliar proofs which could well have been made as experiments by Boys's pupils. It is doubtful that he ever apprenticed his pupils. The arrangement was probably of a more informal nature owing to Boys's own poor financial position. He was evidently still looking for pupils in 1870, as is recorded in a letter written by him which complains of the lack of pupils and his general poverty.[44]

Although he continued to exhibit the reworked views of his youth, there is evidence of a late blossoming of a new style. Two small sepia sketches (Plate 100) from among the works bought at the artist's sale have a confidence in the handling of intimate landscape scenes which shows that Boys had not completely lost his powers of expression. The slightly spiky treatment of the foliage recalls that displayed in the Cowley *Lodge in a Park* (Plate 91). They have a loose, relaxed feeling that must reflect a new-found freedom. This idiom is maintained in a watercolour from the same source depicting a *Washerwoman at the Well* (Plate 101) which is coloured, whereas the other two are purely sepia monochrome. The colouring is high-keyed with its oranges, scarlets, veridian greens and the deep blue of the sky. The rush-like character of the bush above the well is again an immediately recognizable feature of his style, as is the figure of the washer-woman at the right painted in with white bodycolour and vivid scarlet accents. The artist bathes the depths of the well and the crevices of the brickwork with gum to add intensity and give relief to the masonry. These sketches are natural and informal by contrast with the large exhibition watercolours, and though undated it seems likely that they belong to the mid-1860s.

An even later, less precise but more dramatic style emerges in two deeply coloured sketches. The first is a view of a marshy landscape, with almost no features at all, signed with a monogram.[45] He uses the grainy texture of the washes to give the effect of the watery marsh, and uses rough 'Cox' paper which adds to the mood of the picture. It forms a sketch of little consequence, but is an experiment in technique nevertheless. The second (Plate 102), bought at the artist's sale, displays exactly the same treatment of the sky and the use of rough paper. Here the wide range and rich tones of colour recall the scale which he used some forty years earlier in two small landscape sketches. Boys has painted here an almost classical Wilsonesque view, but has given it a drama and sublimity which are far removed from the subtle harmonies of Wilson, or indeed of his own youth. The dark shadows of the cliffs surrounding the lake are bathed with gum, and the foreground is heavily overworked with dry and varied colours. The spiky treatment of the trees parallels that in the *Washerwoman at the Well* (Plate 101). The picture reveals a

60

wealth of feeling for the sublimity of nature, and an almost youthful intensity. Above all it shows that his powers of expression were in no way diminished in the last years of his life.

Boys's remaining years were spent in complete and unremitting misery. On 13 December 1869 he was due to appear before the bankruptcy court in London,[46] but somehow he managed to scrape together enough resources to stave off that fate. Matters did not improve; stories relate that in the last two years of his life he suffered from general paralysis, the most frustrating demise for a creative artist. Finally he died on 10 October 1874. He made no will and it is recorded in the wills register at Somerset House that he had effects of under a hundred pounds. His wife, Célestine, was the sole inheritor as they had no children. It is possible that she went back to Belgium, to her native town of Soignies, after Boys's death. His artist's sale at 30 Acacia Road (where he had died) may have brought her some financial security and at least enabled her to return to her own family in Belgium.

It was a sad end to a long and varied life. It is perhaps a mark of the character of Boys that throughout his long struggle with poverty, and ultimately bankruptcy, he did not sell his most valuable and prized possession, the diamond ring which Louis Philippe had given him. To the end he clung on to the memory of the period of his greatest fame and happiness.

NOTES TO CHAPTER FIVE

1 This is supported by a letter in the collection of Mr and Mrs Cyril Fry which Boys wrote from his temporary lodging at 20 Howland Street on 13 May 1842: 'I have moved & what is much worse I must do so again, for I am comfortable where I am, but a former lodger has stronger claim it appears.'
2 Callow, *op. cit.*, page 73.
3 The ring is described by Henry Scott Boys, and in a letter written to him by Ethel Rigaud Strong Boys on 26 October 1905. Both references are contained in *The Boys Family*, by Guy Ponsonby Boys, in the British Museum, London (Add. 44918).
4 *Terrace of Houses*, watercolour, $10\frac{3}{4} \times 14$ ins/273 × 356 mm., signed: *T. Boys, 1833*, Private Collection, England.
5 *Art Union*, 1842, page 103. Unsold at the exhibition (see Appendix B), this watercolour was later sold as a prize in the Art Union of London—one of the art sweepstakes in fashion in the late 1830s and early '40s. Thomas Boys, the publisher, was to try his own lottery in 1843 (see prospectus preserved in the Bank of England archives and *Lotteries and Sweepstakes*, by C. L'Estrange Ewen, London, 1932, page 299 *passim*).
6 Cooke, *op. cit.*
7 See Appendix B.
8 Private Collection in America. A sketch of Frankfurt is dated 1846. Among the collection of drawings sold as Lot 50 at Christie's on 8 July 1955 were other views of Frankfurt and Leipzig, dated 1846.
9 See Appendix A.
10 The Société Libre des Beaux Arts does not appear to have been a major French exhibiting group, and records of its exhibitions no longer exist.
11 The Société Belge des Aquarellistes is probably the Société royale Belge des Aquarellistes founded in 1856. Boys thus became a member of it relatively late in his life. Records of its exhibitions before 1881 are no longer preserved.
12 Watercolour, $7\frac{3}{4} \times 10\frac{7}{8}$ ins/197 × 276 mm., Private Collection, England.
13 Watercolour, $5\frac{5}{8} \times 8$ ins/143 × 203 mm., inscribed and dated 1844.
14 It is possible that earlier in 1846 Boys made another visit to Darmstadt as there exist tracing-paper drawings of German views dated 1846 (see Note 8 above).
15 Aaron Edwin Penley (1807–70), a prolific painter of portraits and landscapes who also wrote several books on watercolour painting.
16 Henry E. Huntington Library and Art Gallery, San Marino, California (H.M. 16682).
17 See Appendix B. This was a favourite scene with Boys, who painted it at least seven times.
18 He was later to exhibit it at the International Exhibition in 1862 (see Appendix B) even though he had already sold it.
19 *The Art Journal*, page 178.
20 These were Plate XI in *Views of Ancient Monuments in Central America, Chapas and Yucatan*, by F. Catherwood, London, 1844, and Plate V in *Six Views of Kot Kangra and the surrounding country*, by Lieut.-Col. Jack, London, 1847.

21 The lithographs are pulled from the same stones as were used in the 1835 Delpech series (see Groschwitz, *op. cit.,* Check List No. 33). This was a testimony to the way in which drawings on stone could last, but unhappily the sharpness was lost.

22 The volume was published in 1845.

23 Published in London in 1851; see Groschwitz, *op. cit.,* Check List No. 35.

24 Three volumes published in London 1851–53; see Groschwitz, *op. cit.,* Check List No. 37.

25 Preface to *Examples of the Architecture of Venice,* 1851.

26 The *Builder,* No. 417, 1 February 1850, page 83 and thereafter frequently in 1851. As from the advertisement in No. 452, on 4 October his address appears as 18 Albany Street. It seems that Boys began working for architects earlier than 1851, according to three letters in the collection of Mr and Mrs Cyril Fry. These, written in 1848, indicate that Boys was working for an architect named Edward Goodwin, of Lewisham, who was being somewhat backward in paying Boys for his services.

27 See Alastair Smart, 'Cowley Manor in Gloucestershire and some unpublished watercolours from the studio of Thomas Shotter Boys', published in the *Transactions of the Bristol and Gloucestershire Archaeological Society,* Volume XCII, spring 1974, pages 198–201, in which Professor Smart considers the remodelling of the Manor in the 1850s, and compares the actual architecture with that shown in Boys's watercolours; the watercolours are in a Private Collection, England.

28 Buildings designed by Poynter include Christ Church, Westminster (1841); Pynes House, Devon; Castle Melgwyn, South Wales; Hodsock, Nottinghamshire, and restorations at Warwick Castle and Crewe Hall.

29 Private Collection in America.

30 Pencil drawing with sepia wash, $6\frac{1}{2} \times 10\frac{1}{8}$ ins/165 × 257 mm., Private Collection, England.

31 Addressed to Henry Mogford, Secretary of the Winter Exhibition at 121 Pall Mall; now in the Henry E. Huntington Library and Art Gallery, San Marino, California (H.M. 16683).

32 See Appendix B.

33 Guy Ponsonby Boys, *op. cit.,* Volume II, Entry No. 54.

34 See Appendix B. Boys may have made these tours in the company of his pupil Samuel Wilkes who was exhibiting at the Royal Academy in 1857–59.

35 See Appendix B.

36 Watercolour, $8\frac{1}{2} \times 20\frac{3}{4}$ ins/216 × 527 mm., with the Leger Art Galleries, London, 1974. The Victoria and Albert Museum possesses a pencil on tracing-paper view of the same, $7\frac{3}{4} \times 25\frac{1}{2}$ ins/197 × 648 mm., dated 1861 and inscribed *East, or Exhibition Road if reversed* (E.719-1955). It also has a ground plan with measurements. This supports the idea that the watercolour is a realization of the architectural plans, as the Exhibition did not take place until 1862, being postponed from 1861. The building was designed by Captain Francis Fowke of the Royal Engineers, and built on the site of the Natural History Museum; it was pulled down within two years.

37 See Appendix B.

38 Whether Boys paid further visits to his sister and brother-in-law in Darmstadt is impossible to say without documentation, but that he was still in close contact is evidenced by a watercolour he exhibited at the New Water-Colour Society in 1863 — *The Castle of Kranichstein, near Darmstadt* — produced from a sketch by Mr Montague Cooke (his nephew). See Appendix B.

39 See Appendix B.

40 Watercolour, $13\frac{1}{2} \times 20$ ins/343 × 508 mm., signed *Glacier of Bondhuis, Thos. Boys 1860,* Private Collection, England.

41 See Note 38 above.

42 See Note 34 above.

43 Private Collection, England. Another artist who might have been in Boys's studio as an assistant for a period was John Collins Boys, the eldest son of Shotter Boys's cousin Thomas. John's second name was taken from Shotter Boys's mother; he later became an architect and engineer.

44 Information disclosed in a letter written by Mr E. E. Newton of Hampstead in April 1933. See British Museum, London, *Familia Boisiana* (Add. 45500).

45 *Marsh landscape,* watercolour, $3\frac{5}{8} \times 6$ ins/92 × 152 mm., Private Collection, England.

46 *The Times,* 27 November 1869, page 8, column 1.

PLATES

The positions of signatures and inscriptions are
indicated in the captions as follows:

(TL)	top left
(TR)	top right
(BL)	bottom left
(BR)	bottom right
(BC)	bottom centre
(UL)	underneath left
(UR)	underneath right
(UC)	underneath centre

PLATE 1
SCORPION
Watercolour heightened with gum arabic, $5\frac{1}{2} \times 3\frac{7}{8}$ ins/140×99 mm.
Henry E. Huntington Art Gallery, San Marino, California (59.55.115).

PLATE 2
LIZARD
Watercolour heightened with gum arabic, $8\frac{3}{4} \times 6\frac{3}{8}$ ins/223×162 mm.
Henry E. Huntington Art Gallery, San Marino, California (59.55.115).

These two small studies are the earliest works known by Shotter Boys. They are just the type of work that a young apprentice might do in a studio. Drawing animals would have taught Boys to delineate correctly and precisely, and the hand-colouring of this work would have been a preparation for the task of hand-colouring engravings. Here Boys has used gum to add depth to the dark shadowing of the scorpion—proof of his early acquaintance with up-to-date watercolour practice. The two drawings are competent, if uninspired, and serve to show Boys's early facility with the pen and brush.

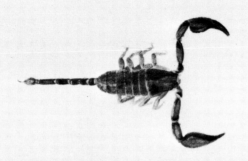

PLATE 3
FUCHSIA GRACILIS

Hand-coloured engraving, $6\frac{5}{8} \times 4\frac{1}{4}$ ins/169 × 108 mm.
Inscribed (BL) T. Boys. del.
       (BR) G.C.sc.
       (BC) Fuchsia gracilis.
Plate 934 in *The Botanical Cabinet* by Conrad Loddiges & Sons, Volume X, London, 1824.

PLATE 4
CAMELLIA SASANQUA

Hand-coloured engraving, $8 \times 6\frac{1}{4}$ ins/203 × 159 mm.
Inscribed (BL) T. Boys del.
       (BC) Camellia sasanqua pleno-carneo.
Plate 1134 in *The Botanical Cabinet* by Conrad Loddiges & Sons, Volume XII, London, 1826.

These finely executed hand-coloured engravings are just two of the many that Boys did for *The Botanical Cabinet* between 1824 and 1833. The book was a George Cooke studio production and it is likely that Boys was working on it right from the first volume, issued in 1818. However, at that early stage Boys was still an apprentice and so his name does not appear on the plates. Others working on the project included E. W. Cooke, W. J. Cooke, Jane Loddiges (E. W. Cooke's future wife), G. and W. Loddiges, W. Miller and a Miss Rebello. These botanical draughtsmen drew the plants, which were then engraved by George Cooke, and subsequently hand-coloured, possibly also by the same draughtsmen. The colouring is remarkably delicate and naturalistic, just as the underlying drawing is botanically correct and precise in its outlines and light in its shading. It was this sort of work that would have built up Boys's capacity for careful draughtsmanship and the control of wash and tone.

Camellia *Maddnskin* *Vctor* 1770.

Fuchsia gracilis.

PLATE 5

LES SALINIERES BY TROUVILLE, by Richard Parkes Bonington (1803–28)

Watercolour, $4\frac{1}{4} \times 8\frac{3}{4}$ ins/108 × 222 mm.

Inscribed (Verso) <u>Drawn for me by R. P. Bonington</u>
<u>to show me the place of Chancre,</u>
<u>1826, Rue des Martyrs. Thos. S.</u>
<u>Boys.</u>

Private Collection, England.

Photograph by courtesy of the Manning Gallery, London.

PLATE 6

LES SALINIERES BY TROUVILLE

Watercolour, $3\frac{3}{4} \times 7\frac{3}{8}$ ins/95 × 187 mm.

Private Collection, England.

PLATE 7

LES SALINIERES BY TROUVILLE, by Richard Parkes Bonington

Oil on millboard, $8\frac{1}{2} \times 13\frac{1}{2}$ ins/216 × 343 mm.

The National Gallery of Scotland.

This interesting group of pictures provides evidence of the close collaboration between Boys and Bonington as early as 1826. Whether Bonington painted his watercolour *en plein air* or in the studio specifically at Boys's request is difficult to determine. However, it does appear that the Boys watercolour and Bonington's oil painting were painted on the same day, the two artists sitting close to each other. The atmosphere of both pictures is similar, contrasting with that in Bonington's watercolour, and the two artists have both painted in the smoking chimney of the cottage in the background. Boys's watercolour does not yet exhibit the fluidity of Bonington's, but it is hardly the work of a newcomer to the medium. The warm autumnal tones are skilfully handled with the accents of burnt scarlet and green to add appropriate highlights. Above all it exhibits a freedom and spontaneity which testifies to his natural and sensitive talents as a watercolourist.

68

PLATE 8
JUMIEGES, by Richard Parkes Bonington (1803–28)
Watercolour, $8\frac{3}{4} \times 12\frac{1}{8}$ ins/222 × 308 mm.
Private Collection, England.

PLATE 9
JUMIEGES

Watercolour, $4\frac{3}{4} \times 7\frac{1}{8}$ ins/121 × 181 mm.
Inscribed (BR) Jumieges
Private Collection, USA.

Dr Marion Spencer ascribes the Bonington watercolour to a date of around 1825. Boys was certainly in close contact with Bonington at that date, so it is not surprising to find them sketching together in the French countryside. Boys's picture was painted from a point just to the right of Bonington's and from a slightly higher viewpoint. In style these two watercolours are very similar, particularly in the brief handling of the landscape in quick and loosely controlled washes. Bonington's work is more highly coloured and the masses of the trees are more powerfully realized than in that by Boys, which is less adventurous. The sweep of the trees in the Bonington gives it a direction which the more diffuse Boys does not possess. Boys's heavy use of crayon on the bush at the right was probably inspired by Bonington's use of dark colour in the foreground to indicate the side of the grassy bank. Bonington makes powerful use of the rough paper to add light and texture to the foreground. Technically less commendable, Boys's work documents his early intimacy with and reliance on Bonington in both style and colouring.

PLATE 10
LE PONT DE LA CONCORDE WITH THE TUILERIES IN THE DISTANCE

Watercolour heightened with bodycolour, $5\frac{1}{4} \times 8\frac{1}{8}$ ins/133×206 mm.
Private Collection, England.

PLATE 11
LE PONT DE LA CONCORDE WITH THE TUILERIES IN THE DISTANCE, by Richard Parkes Bonington (1803–28)

Watercolour, 5×8 ins/127×203 mm.
Signed (BR) R P B
Private Collection, England.

At first glance one might think that Boys had copied the watercolour by Bonington, yet on closer study the reverse seems more likely. The details in the Bonington are loose and ambiguous; the middle distance lacks conviction, and the drawing of the coach to the left is imprecise. Boys's drawing is more correct and has the feeling of having been painted from nature. By comparison, Bonington's work has the uncertain air of a copy. If this is so, it means that both were painted by 1828, the year of Bonington's death. Possibly Bonington, chairbound with tuberculosis, copied a watercolour which Boys had done.

Boys's watercolour lacks the controlled washes and the solidity of his work of the 1830s; the paint is mixed and does not have the granular texture which is a major characteristic of his later style. The use of the bodycolour, touched-in rather clumsily, is the mark of an artist who has not yet mastered his medium. Boningtonian in conception, it marks a comparatively early stage in his development as a water-colourist. An undated view of the *Old Hôtel de Ville, St Omer*, $9\frac{1}{2} \times 7\frac{1}{4}$ ins/241×184 mm., in the Nottingham Castle Museum, exhibits a similar inconsistency in technique suggesting an equally early date, and it must certainly have been painted before 1831 as the Hôtel de Ville at St Omer was pulled down in that year (though this did not prevent Boys from repeating this subject often throughout his life).

PLATE 12
THE PONT DES ARTS, PARIS
Watercolour, $6\frac{5}{8} \times 13\frac{3}{8}$ ins/168 × 340 mm.
Inscribed (BC and, cut off, TR) Pont des Arts, Paris
Collection of Mr and Mrs Paul Mellon.

PLATE 13
ROUEN
Watercolour, $13\frac{1}{8} \times 18\frac{3}{4}$ ins/334 × 475 mm.
Whitworth Art Gallery, University of Manchester (D. 4.1905).

These are two riverscapes from a relatively early period in Boys's career; one exhibits a closeness in style to Bonington, the other a divergence in both technique and conception. The Rouen painting was in fact attributed to Bonington up until 1939. Boningtonian in composition, it is treated in a more precise manner than is typical of Bonington himself. The massing of the trees at the left is slightly clumsy but elsewhere the painting is superbly and confidently handled (c.f. Figure XVI). The unfinished *Pont des Arts* was stopped at the stage where Boys had worked in the local tints in the background before going on to the detail.

74

PLATE 14
HOTEL DE BELLEVUE AND CAFE D'AMITIE SEEN FROM THE PARK, BRUSSELS

Watercolour, $6\frac{3}{4} \times 10\frac{1}{2}$ ins/172 × 267 mm.

Signed (BC) T. Boys. 1830.

Inscribed (Verso) Hotel de Bellevue and Café d'Amitié seen from the Park, Brussels, from the collection of William Wells,[1] Redleaf Park, Kent.

Private Collection, England.

This picture provides proof that Boys was in Brussels during the Belgian Revolution in the summer of 1830. It is of historical importance as an 'on-the-spot' depiction of life during the Revolution. Despite what must have been a turbulent time, Boys has pictured a tranquil scene, disturbed only by the exercising of the soldiers. The building to the right seems to have been damaged; the balustrade has been blown away in one place.

The paint has been brushed on in dragged washes of varying shades of brown, relieved by judicious dashes of blue and red, deftly touched on to enliven the total effect. Although skilful in its handling of the forms and the surface texture of the sunlit masonry, the subtle three-dimensional forms of the statue at the right seem to have eluded him.

---

[1] William Wells was one of the leading patrons of the early nineteenth century, and numbered Turner and Constable among his artist friends. It is interesting to know that he also possessed a work by Boys.

PLATE 15
L'INSTITUT DE FRANCE

Watercolour, $14 \times 10\frac{7}{8}$ ins/355×276 mm.
Signed (BC) Thomas Boys/1830
Collection of Mr and Mrs Paul Mellon.

Directly comparable to the view by Bonington (Figure II), this watercolour shows the difference between the two artists in both their approach to the scene and in their respective styles. Bonington's watercolour is treated much more atmospherically, with less attention to the actual forms and details of the scene. He daringly placed a woman sitting on a block of masonry in the foreground, her clothes a violent scarlet, which brings a touch of intimacy to the scene. Boys retains the grandeur of the building, both by his composition and by the cool and deliberate colouring. Boys's composition is carefully constructed to lead the eye into depth by way of the barrels, the blocks of masonry, the cart being pulled up towards the courtyard of the Institut and so to the bridge. The luminosity of the background buildings on the Ile de la Cité provides a perfect foil to the robust lines of the Institut with its solid browns and blues. The azure sky, made up of horizontal washes, complements the warm tones of the ground and the architecture. Refined and purposeful, this watercolour contradicts the principles inherent in Bonington's depiction of the same scene.

78

PLATE 16
THE SEINE AND THE TUILERIES

Watercolour, $7\frac{7}{8} \times 11\frac{5}{8}$ ins/200 × 295 mm.
Signed (BR) Boys
The Tate Gallery, London (T. 966).

In this watercolour Boys has outdone Girtin (Figure XIV). He has maintained Girtin's accuracy of depiction without his mannerisms of line. Girtin's etchings are airless and dry. In Boys's work the whole scene is pervaded with a natural and vivacious atmosphere. The colour tone and texture are controlled superbly, from the cool blues of the houses at the left and the sunbathed beige tones of the Louvre, to the touches of hot scarlet in the figures. The cool azure sky provides a perfect backdrop to the scene, complementing but not overwhelming it.

PLATE 17
VERSAILLES

Watercolour, $5 \times 7\frac{1}{4}$ ins/127×184 mm.
Collection of Mr and Mrs Paul Mellon.

PLATE 18
VERSAILLES

Watercolour, $7\frac{1}{4} \times 10\frac{1}{4}$ ins/183×261 mm.
Private Collection, England.

These two watercolours were painted during the early 1830s, when Boys was making sketching visits to Versailles with Callow. The first picture is of a type which is all too scarce in Boys's early period—the quick, fluent and impressionistic sketch made on the spot. It was subsequently worked up, with variations, to form the finished picture. The treatment of the first recalls that of *Jumièges* (Plate 9) with its broad use of a single wash and its dark pencil/crayon work over the watercolour to indicate trees. It is a tremendously atmospheric work whose mood contrasts strongly with the finished watercolour, which is more restrained and pastoral in character. Boys has used a degree of artistic licence in the finished watercolour; he has brought the palace closer to the spectator, making it more monumental. He has changed the construction of the foreground, putting in a leafy sapling and a stile with a figure leaning on it looking at the people by the lake. Cleverly constructed, this building-up of the left-hand foreground balances the mass of the palace, correcting the uneasy composition in the preparatory watercolour. These two watercolours display to full advantage the very different facets of Boys's style in the period immediately after Bonington's death.

82

PLATE 19
VERSAILLES

Watercolour, $6\frac{1}{8} \times 8\frac{3}{4}$ ins/156 × 222 mm.
Private Collection, England.
Photograph by courtesy of Christie's, London.

This work contrasts with the two previous plates in its depiction of Versailles. The other two were taken from nature and were factual representations of the appearance of the Palace in the early 1830s. Here Boys is imagining a scene from the past. The Palace architecture is briefly and schematically indicated in the background. In the foreground is a group of figures in 'Van Dyck' costume, painted with a brilliance and feeling for the texture of cloth not normally seen in Boys's work. The whole scene is invested with a transient atmosphere further amplified by the delicate balustrade on the right and the evanescent puffs of foliage that form the trees. This is one of Boys's few excursions into what may be called history painting, but still the emphasis is very much on the landscape and architecture rather than on the figures. This experiment was perhaps inspired by Boys's familiarity with Bonington's historical works.

PLATE 20
NOTRE DAME, PARIS
Watercolour heightened with bodycolour and gum arabic, $15\frac{1}{8} \times 11\frac{5}{16}$ ins/383×287 mm.
Signed Thos. Boys./1832.
Fondation Custodia, Institut Néerlandais, Paris (1971.T.39).

This watercolour represents a maturity of style which differs from the rather evanescent qualities of his earlier pictures. An essay in grey with subtle gradations of tone, it is so different from some of the more sparkling colours of the broadly contemporary *Seine and the Tuileries* (Plate 16). He delights in contrasting the tints and granular textures of each wash. Touches such as the gum on the coat of the central figure, the scratched whites and warm reds and blues of the shirts and caps are simply embellishments to set off the greys.

Boys copied this watercolour four years later, creating a very different mood.[1] Whereas the washes here are measured and controlled, in the later version the treatment is wetter and more violent, the washes in the sky giving the effect of a storm. The washes have a sepia tone and there is heavy overdrawing, also in sepia. The figures too are altered, with two stretcher-bearers moving towards the hospital at the left, adding a note of local colour.

[1]Watercolour, $9\frac{3}{4} \times 7\frac{1}{16}$ ins/247×180 mm., signed (CL) T. Boys. 1836. Victoria and Albert Museum, London (D. 1588–1907).

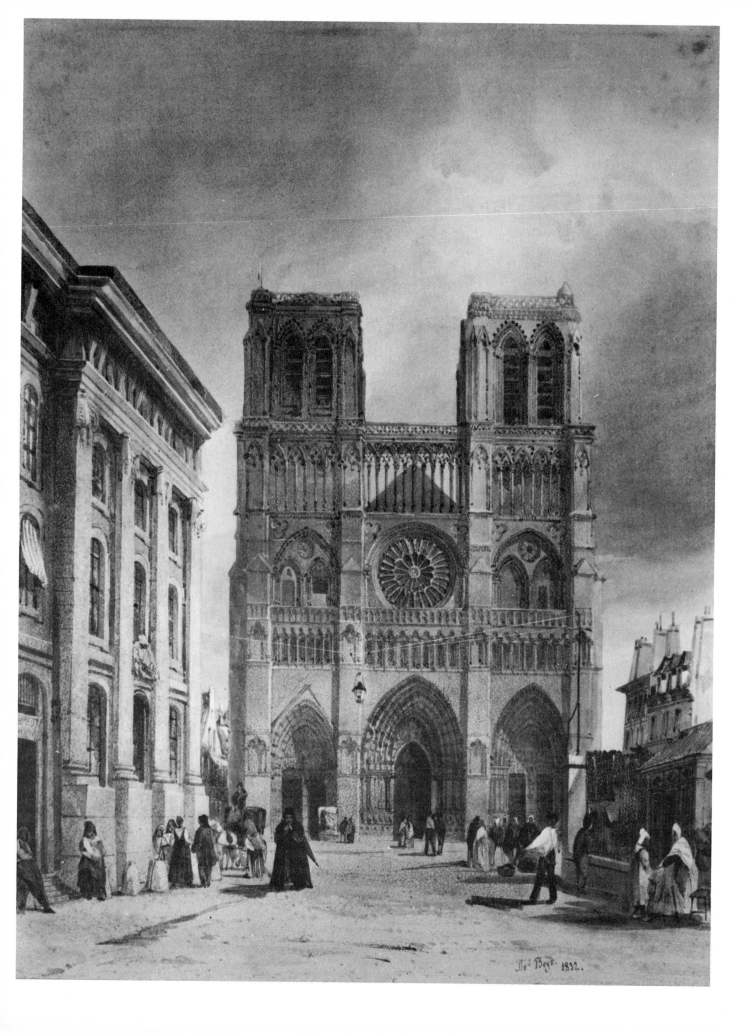

PLATE 21

VIEW OF THE PONT ROYAL AND THE TUILERIES FROM THE INSTITUTE, PARIS

Pencil drawing, $9\frac{1}{2} \times 12\frac{1}{2}$ ins/242 × 318 mm.
Inscribed (BR) Pont Royal from the Institute
The National Gallery of Canada, Ottawa (6038).

PLATE 22

VIEW OF THE PONT ROYAL AND THE TUILERIES FROM THE INSTITUTE, PARIS

Watercolour heightened with gum arabic, $9\frac{3}{4} \times 14$ ins/248 × 356 mm.
Signed (BL) Thos. Boys/1832.
Private Collection, England.

One of the few pencil drawings from this early French period still in existence, Plate 21 contrasts with the precise style displayed in *Le Pont Royal et le quai d'Orsay* (Plate 23). There is barely enough information in the drawing from which to build up the watercolour. One suspects that Boys may have had another drawing and a wash sketch to aid him. He has pulled the whole scene together in a composition which defies all the rules of painting. The picture is divided into two halves, and in the final watercolour pivots round the central point of the woman in the foreground. The disposition of the figures is carefully placed so as to help the cohesion of the scene and lead through to the distant view. The massive form of the Institut is balanced by the bank of cloud building up at the right. The delicacy of the colours, with their pale blues and beiges, is complemented by the touches of orange and scarlet in the figures.

88

PLATE 23
LE PONT ROYAL ET LE QUAI D'ORSAY, PARIS

Pencil on two pieces of paper, $10\frac{1}{2} \times 9\frac{3}{4}$ ins/266 × 248 mm.

Inscribed (BR) Pont Royal & Quai D'Orsai Sepr 1833.

      (Pencil note on logs, CL) wood.

Fondation Custodia, Institut Néerlandais, Paris (1971.T.21).

This attractive drawing with its precise and detailed treatment of the architecture gives a clue concerning Boys's drawing methods. The broad expanse of the sky and the foreground are very realistic, so much so as to exclude any hint of artistic licence. The overall character is mechanical, and it seems very possible that it was made with the help of an instrument such as the Graphic Telescope, used by Cornelius Varley. The lifeless quality of this drawing is emphasized when one compares it with the contemporary drawing of *L'Institut* (Plate 26). Few drawings of this type survive from Boys's *oeuvre*, but it is probable that they formed the basis of his watercolours and his lithographs. In its concentration of line, with little attempt to portray the tones and textures of nature, it would have provided a good framework from which he could improvise.

Pont Royal et Quai d'Orsay   6.ᵉ 1833.

PLATE 24

**L'INSTITUT AND L'ISLE DE LA CITE FROM
THE QUAI DU LOUVRE,** by Richard Parkes Bonington (1803–28)

Watercolour heightened with bodycolour, $6 \times 8\frac{3}{4}$ ins/152 × 222 mm.
Signed (BR) RPB. 1828
Private Collection, England.

PLATE 25

**L'INSTITUT AND L'ISLE DE LA CITE FROM
THE QUAI DU LOUVRE,** by William Callow (1812–1908)

Pencil, $9 \times 19\frac{3}{5}$ ins/229 × 499 mm.
Inscribed (BL) Paris from the Tuilleries/Saturday May 28th 1831

      (BC) L'Institute, Mai 31st 1831

      Pencil colour notes and instructions.
Victoria and Albert Museum, London (E. 862–1937).
Reproduced by courtesy of the Victoria and Albert Museum.

PLATE 26

L'INSTITUT AND L'ISLE DE LA CITE FROM THE QUAI DU LOUVRE

Pencil on tracing paper, $9\frac{9}{16} \times 19\frac{15}{16}$ ins/243 × 507 mm.
Inscribed (BR) L'Institut l'isle de la cité from the quai du Louvre.

      Pencil colour notes.
British Museum, London (1952.5.10.33).
Reproduced by courtesy of the Trustees of the British Museum.

For discussion of these three plates see under Plate 27.

PLATE 27
L'INSTITUT AND L'ISLE DE LA CITE FROM THE QUAI DU LOUVRE

Watercolour heightened with bodycolour and gum arabic, $6\frac{1}{2} \times 10\frac{3}{4}$ ins/165×273 mm.
Signed (BC) Thomas Boys/1833
Fondation Custodia (Coll. Fritz Lugt), Institut Néerlandais, Paris.

Another Paris view popular with English artists, which Bonington depicted (Plate 24) in a magnificently atmospheric watercolour. He drew it from a position in the road, whereas Callow (Plate 25) stood on the pavement at the left and concentrated on the Ile de la Cité and the Institut. Bonington's picture, with the road stretching into the distance, is more concerned with what is at the left-hand side. Callow's has no real focus, nor does the Boys tracing (Plate 26) which was taken directly from the former. In his watercolour of 1833 Boys introduced figures and coaches to give direction and cohesion to the scene, and, if anything, his focus is at the right where the Seine disappears between Notre Dame and the Institut. Bonington's architecture and people are rather ethereal. Boys's architecture is more precisely executed in both the drawing and the application of watercolour. These two watercolours emphasize the different qualities of each artist, and how Boys, though influenced by Bonington in both composition and technique, had a style and conception of art that was far removed from that of Bonington.

The introduction of the coaches and the promenading figures on the left in the Boys so closely parallels the same features in the Bonington that it seems probable that Boys knew or perhaps owned the Bonington. The process of copying a Callow drawing so precisely (itself perhaps inspired in style by Boys's drawing technique) to form the basis of his own watercolour is evidence of the close association between the two, attested by Callow himself, when they shared a studio in the Rue du Bouloy. Copying did not prevent Boys from improvising the figures and vehicles, giving character and emphasis to the work. Given the freshness and vivid light of the picture, it is likely that Boys painted the watercolour *en plein air*.

94

Thomas Daniell 1833

PLATE 28
BOULEVARD DES ITALIENS, PARIS
Watercolour heightened with bodycolour and gum arabic, $14\frac{5}{8} \times 23\frac{1}{2}$ ins/372×597 mm.
Signed (BR) Thos. Boys/1833
British Museum, London (1870.10.8.2364).
Reproduced by courtesy of the Trustees of the British Museum.

This watercolour is larger than others by Boys from this period yet, unlike most of his other watercolours, it does not suffer from lack of control. The colours are marvellously balanced, with the delicate tinting and overworking of bright emerald and red bodycolour. The white dress of the woman in the centre of the picture is scratched out allowing the brilliant white of the paper to show through. The figures are beautifully drawn and show a great range of the social spectrum. The blue of the sky is complemented by the introduction of yellow wisps of cloud and the grey haze of the horizon. This watercolour must have been one of his major works of the early 1830s and displays to the full the heights which he had attained by this stage.

PLATE 29
FRENCH COASTAL SCENE WITH TWO CHILDREN
Watercolour, $4\frac{1}{2} \times 7\frac{3}{4}$ ins/114 × 197 mm.
Signed (BR) T. Boys/1830
Collection of Mr J. Wyatt-Williams.

PLATE 30
LANDSCAPE WITH CHURCH STEEPLE IN THE DISTANCE
Watercolour, $2\frac{5}{6} \times 5\frac{7}{8}$ ins/71 × 149 mm.
Signed (BL) T. B. 1834
Albany Gallery, London, 1974.
Photograph by courtesy of the Albany Gallery.

From these two slight sketches one can see that Boys's natural ability did not only lie in large and detailed watercolours. The coastal scene, painted in broad easy washes swept across the paper, shows a delicacy of colour and treatment which is sometimes obscured in his larger works. The two children in the foreground are typically Boysian, if unintentionally humorous in their exaggerated proportions.

The landscape, though a sketch, is treated with considerable variation in brushwork: he employs dry granular washes, thin transparent glazes, wet daubs of colour dropped into a drying wash in the foliage, and uses his thumb to texture the edges of the trees. It is a clever watercolour with its warm autumnal tones accented by cool blue in the background and balanced by red touches in the figures and the signature.

FRENCH PORT SCENE
Watercolour heightened with bodycolour, $6\frac{3}{8} \times 11\frac{1}{4}$ ins/162 × 286 mm.
Henry E. Huntington Art Gallery, San Marino, California (59.55.112).

This watercolour shows a very subtle gradation of tone, from the pale blue of the sky to the light grey of the roofs of the town. The washes are used thinly to convey each nuance of colour, and the drawing is delicately done in order not to dominate the tones. Touches of white bodycolour pick out the figures promenading along the estuary. Boys has not employed any elaborate compositional devices and relies purely on a screen of consecutive horizontal washes and forms to lead the eye into depth.

PLATE 32
VIEW OF PARIS AND THE SEINE FROM BERCY
Watercolour, $7\frac{1}{8} \times 11\frac{7}{8}$ ins/181 × 302 mm.
Private Collection, England.

Another view often painted by English artists working in Paris, it can be compared to a pencil drawing by Callow of a similar view taken from the other side of the pavilion (Figure III). This watercolour is unusual in Boys's *oeuvre* because of its high-keyed intensity of tone and its dramatic use of the long evening shadows. The warmth of the sunset permeates every part of the composition and the overall orange colour is contrasted by the cool veridian green of the tree on the right. It is easy to see in this work how Boys worked up his foregrounds by breaking up the colour, adding different tints of the same colour in the shadows, dropping dry washes over underlying granular tints and adding random dots of scarlet to draw attention to the foreground, pushing the background into relief. The picture has the expressiveness and grandeur of a Turner, and a particularly Turneresque touch are the long shadows of the dogs in the foreground.

PLATE 33
ST ALPHAGE FROM THE PARK, GREENWICH
Watercolour, $8\frac{1}{8} \times 6\frac{1}{2}$ ins/207 × 166 mm.
Signed (BL) T Boys 1831.
British Museum, London (1944.10.14.23).
Reproduced by courtesy of the Trustees of the British Museum.

PLATE 34
GREENWICH HOSPITAL FROM THE PARK
Watercolour heightened with bodycolour, $5 \times 7\frac{3}{4}$ ins/ 127 × 197 mm.
Signed (BL) T Boys/1830
Private Collection, England.

These two watercolours were executed during Boys's visits to England in the early 1830s. At that stage he was resident in Paris and these watercolours formed an interlude in the development of his watercolour style in France. They display a variety of brushwork; both exhibit the technique of scumbling dragged colour over the underlying washes to create the flickering shadows under the trees. To portray the deer in the St Alphage view he scratched away the forms and then delicately dropped in warm browns for local colouring. In the 1830 view he was more concerned with the mass of the trees while in the 1831 watercolour he pays more attention to the individual character of the foliage.

104

PLATE 35
LAMB ROW, CHESTER

Watercolour, $6\frac{1}{4} \times 9$ ins/159×228 mm.
Signed (BR) T Boys/1833
Grosvenor Museum, Chester (9.a.52).

PLATE 36
LAMB ROW, CHESTER

Watercolour, $8\frac{1}{2} \times 10\frac{1}{2}$ ins/216×267 mm.
Signed (BL) T. Boys . . .
Private Collection, England.

These two watercolours must have been painted on Boys's visit to England in 1833. There are no other watercolours known of Chester from that year, so it is unlikely that his stay there was of any duration. Obviously he was fascinated by this old tumble-down house in Lamb Row, so much so that he painted it from both sides. He relishes the picturesque irregularity of its features, virtually filling the whole picture space with this one building. It is interesting to compare the different character and atmosphere of the two versions, and the appropriateness of the carts and figures introduced into each.

106

PLATE 37
THE CASTLE MILLS AND BRIDGE OVER THE FOSS AT YORK

Pencil and watercolour, $4\frac{3}{8} \times 7\frac{1}{8}$ ins/111 × 181 mm.
Signed (BL) T. Boys 1833.
Collection Mr and Mrs Paul Mellon.

PLATE 38
THE CASTLE MILLS AND BRIDGE OVER THE FOSS AT YORK

Watercolour, $7\frac{1}{8} \times 10\frac{5}{8}$ ins/181 × 270 mm.
Signed (BR) T. Boys/1833
Whitworth Art Gallery, Manchester (D. 23.1933).

The Mellon work is obviously a preparatory sketch for the Whitworth watercolour. It seems likely that it was the only source of information for the final watercolour. The pencil drawing is brief, but sufficient, and Boys has added little to it in the final version. The washes in the Mellon version indicate the tones and the barest colours. In the finished watercolour Boys has largely kept the tonal composition of the preliminary work. The one significant change is in the house at the left which he has lightened to give better body to the architecture. The final colours in the watercolour are orange and grey for the most part, and lacking the true freshness of colour of a work painted *en plein air*. It has the slightly laboured air of a studio work. The figures are improvised in the second version to give to the composition a cohesion which it lacked in the sketch.

PLATE 39
VUE DE ROUEN

Soft-ground etching, $7\frac{1}{16} \times 6\frac{3}{16}$ ins/180 × 157 mm.
Signed (BL) <u>Thos Boys/1833</u> (the first 3 is reversed).
The Albert P. Strietmann Collection, Cincinnati Art Museum, Ohio.

This is one of the five soft-ground etchings that Boys made in or around 1833.[1] They were not published and were presumably just experiments with a new medium that he was anxious to try. Although the characteristics of a line drawing are maintained, the actual drawing is less precise than in his watercolours and lithographs. He depicts here one of the crumbling and picturesque streets for which Rouen is famed and introduces touches of humour with the figures. This amusing little exercise evidently delighted him as he bothered to date it. However, he was not encouraged to use soft-ground etching as a method for executing his engraving commissions.

[1] See Chapter 3, page 39.

PLATE 40
ABBEVILLE

Lithograph, 10 × 14 ins/254 × 356 mm.
Inscribed (UL) T. Boys Lithog.
(UR) Imprimé par C. Hullmandel.
(UC) Abbeville/Picardie
Plate in *Voyages Pittoresques et Romantiques dans l'ancienne France,* by J. Taylor, C.H. Nodier and Alp. de Cailleux; *Picardie,* Volume I, Paris, 1835.
Reproduced from the copy in the University Library, Cambridge.

This work displays a mastery and confidence in the basic techniques of lithography. The drawing is controlled, perhaps tending towards generalization in the trees. The ducks in the foreground are a feature which Boys was to make use of again in *London as it is* (Plate 68). The rural air of this scene is a welcome contrast to Boys's more usual preoccupation in this series with architectural themes.

PLATE 41
PLACE DU GRAND MARCHE D'ABBEVILLE

Lithograph, $10\frac{3}{16} \times 14\frac{1}{4}$ ins/259 × 362 mm.

Signed (BR) T Boys

Inscribed (UL) T. Boys lithog.

(UR) Imprimé par C. Hullmandel.

(UC) Place du grand marché d'Abbeville

Plate in *Voyages Pittoresques*;[1] *Picardie,* Volume I.

Reproduced from the copy in the University Library, Cambridge.

Here is a characteristically Boysian scene: picturesque architecture, a variety of people, carts, animals and shop-signs. Boys pulls all these features together to form a coherent composition of the market-place at Abbeville. The mastery of tone and drawing is evident, as is the easy disposition of darks and lights. He skilfully employs the grainy texture of the lithographic stone to give the feeling of the paved road and the mediaeval masonry. The balance between the drawing and tones, and their disposition throughout the lithograph underline the difference in technique between Boys and Bonington, as exemplified in Bonington's *Rue du Gros-Horloge, Rouen* (Figure XV).

[1] *Op. cit.*

114

PLATE 42
RATISBONNE

Lithograph, $10\frac{5}{8} \times 7\frac{9}{16}$ ins/270 × 192 mm.
Signed (BR) T BOYS in reverse.
Inscribed (UL) T. Boys del.
       (UR) Lith de Delpech
Plate XXI in *Architecture pittoresque dessinée d'après nature par A. Rouargue et T. Boys,* Paris, 1835.
Photograph by courtesy of the Albany Gallery, London.

PLATE 43
VIEILLE RUE DU TEMPLE
Vue de l'Hôtel où fut assassiné Louis de France, Duc d'Orléans en 1407.
Lithograph, $9\frac{15}{16} \times 7$ ins/252 × 178 mm.
Signed (BR) T Boys.
Inscribed (UL) T. Boys del
       (UR) Lith. de Delpech A Paris
Plate XLIV in *Architecture pittoresque dessinée d'après nature par A. Rouargue et T. Boys,* Paris, 1835.
Photograph by courtesy of the Albany Gallery, London.

These are two of the lithographs which Boys produced for Delpech's publication of 1835 and it is interesting to compare them in technique and effect to the lithographs printed by Hullmandel in England in the same year. The drawing is very delicate but the tones lack the mass and contrast of those printed by Hullmandel. Nevertheless, they are charming views with characteristic pieces of genre introduced in the activities of the figures.

Samuel Prout painted a watercolour of *Ratisbon Cathedral* (Figure XVIII) from exactly the same spot as Boys drew this lithograph. Prout's drawing is overcrowded with fussy architectural detail and statuesque figures. There are slight differences in the architectural details; Prout over-elaborates and has elongated the proportions, especially in the background.

Boys produced a smaller and narrower version of the *Vieille Rue du Temple* in his 1839 series of chromo-lithographs.[1] As was his custom, he changed the composition of the figures in the later work.

[1] Plate XXII in *Picturesque Architecture in Paris,* London, 1839.

PLATE 44
L'EGLISE DE L'ABBAYE DE MAGUELONNE
Lithograph with touches of lithotint, $13\frac{1}{2} \times 10\frac{3}{8}$ ins/343 × 263 mm.
Inscribed (UL) T Boys lithog
    (UR) Imprimé par C. Hullmandel
    (UC) Eglise de l'Abbaye de Maguelonne./Languedoc
Plate 254 in *Voyages Pittoresques: Languedoc,* Volume II, Part II, 1837.
Reproduced from the copy in the University Library, Cambridge.

This lithograph shows just how advanced was Boys's understanding of the techniques of lithography and its more recent inventions—lithotint, stumping and brush-biting. The variation in tones and textures in this view are a lithographic *tour de force.* Boys focuses the whole composition on the sharp contrast between the dark habit of the monk and the white light on the block of masonry in the foreground. This is a work of minute observation and sensitive execution.

PLATE 45
AT SWISS COTTAGE

PLATE 45
AT SWISS COTTAGE

Watercolour, $3\frac{3}{8} \times 4\frac{3}{4}$ ins/86 × 121 mm.
Signed (BL) T BOYS/1831
Private Collection, England.
Photograph by courtesy of the Albany Gallery, London.

PLATE 46
AT SWISS COTTAGE

Watercolour, $6\frac{15}{16} \times 10\frac{5}{16}$ ins/176 × 270 mm.
Signed (BC) T. Boys 1836
Collection of Mr and Mrs Paul Mellon.

Nearly every Parisian scene painted by Boys in the early 1830s was 'copied' by him and kept for possible future use. The slight sketch of 1831 illustrated here is perhaps the last subject of which one would expect him to make a copy. It is not known whether Boys retained the first sketch in his studio, from which he worked up the 1836 picture which is twice the size of the sketch. The 1836 watercolour is not an exact copy and Boys has allowed himself artistic licence. He has changed the disposition of the figures and the background, adding a wall, some more figures and another tree. The cottage's perspective disappears steeply and the trees are given more substance and form.

PLATE 47
CHATEAU ESPAGNOL NEAR BRUSSELS
Watercolour heightened with gum arabic, $7\frac{1}{8} \times 10\frac{1}{2}$ ins/181 × 267 mm.
Inscribed (Verso) Chateau Espagnol pres de Lacken.
Henry E. Huntington Art Gallery, San Marino, California (59.55.107).

This fluently painted watercolour catches clearly the small country château sitting amongst its protective clump of trees as the afternoon sun casts heavy shadows under its turrets. The pencil details of the architecture under the washes are brief, but are allowed to show through the transparent tints of colour to give the right amount of emphasis to the forms of the building. The watercolour is freely painted with greens and browns in broad, fluent washes. Colour was touched on top of the still-damp underwashes to give the rather blotchy effect of the trees and the grass in the foreground. On the tree at the left Boys's finger-prints are clearly to be seen. Perhaps painted during one of his visits to Belgium in the early 1830s, this is an example of Boys's free sketching style.

QUAI DE LA GREVE, PARIS

Watercolour, $11\frac{1}{4} \times 15\frac{5}{8}$ ins/286×397 mm.
Signed (BC) <u>Thomas Boys/1837.</u>
Victoria and Albert Museum, London (456–1882).
Crown copyright reserved.

This must have been one of the last watercolours that Boys painted in Paris before returning to England in 1837. He employs all the familiar techniques, such as scratching out the whites, adding gum to the bodycolour and overworking the textures of his surfaces. The whole composition is refined in its realization, with the sharp and clear background a major feature.

PLATE 49
L'HOTEL DE SENS, PARIS
Watercolour heightened with bodycolour, $11\frac{5}{8} \times 8\frac{5}{8}$ ins/295 × 219 mm.
Signed (BL) Thos Boys/1833.
Also old signature <u>Thomas Boys</u> . . . scratched out above.
Carnavalet Museum, Paris (d.8482).

Shotter Boys obviously adored this building, making many and varied versions of it both in watercolour and in lithography. This watercolour probably is the first, from which all the later versions were derived. Boys always maintained the same viewpoint of the building, which was different from Callow's version (Figure IV). Painting from this angle, Boys invests the scene with a grandeur that is missing in the Callow.

The building had some significance during the 1830 Revolution and the glorious three days. Above the doorway the masonry is incised with the lettering '29 Juillet 1830' in both Callow's and Boys's works. Boys has also added to the scene the tricolor with its bright blue and red. This watercolour exhibits Boys's method of working up his paintings: scratching away the washes to give texture to the masonry, overlaying dots and dashes of wash to give substance to the ground and dabbing the tints of the sky with a cloth to achieve an even gradation in the washes.

126

PLATE 50
L'HOTEL DE SENS, PARIS

Lithograph, $11\frac{1}{8} \times 5\frac{7}{8}$ ins/283 × 149 mm.
Signed (BL) T. Boys.
      (On block of masonry on cart) T.B.
Inscribed (UL) T. BOYS del
     (UR) Lith. de Delpech
Plate XLII in *Architecture pittoresque dessinée d'après nature par A. Rouargue et T. Boys*, Paris, 1835.
Photograph by courtesy of the Albany Gallery, London.

PLATE 51
L'HOTEL DE SENS, PARIS

Pencil and wash,[1] $11\frac{7}{16} \times 8\frac{9}{16}$ ins/290 × 217 mm.
Carnavalet Museum, Paris (D. 165).
Photograph by Lauros-Giraudon.

The pencil and wash drawing was probably traced from the watercolour of 1833 (Plate 49) and then over-drawn to emphasize the lines: the result is rather artificial. This drawing provides the experimental working ground for the 1835 lithograph. There are minor changes to the architectural detail in the lithograph, giving more detail to the individual blocks of masonry and elaborating the cobbled road. As was his custom, Boys improvises the figural composition, sketching in the preparatory wash drawing a series of ideas, experimenting in an informal manner. The drawing thus provides an insight into Boys's method of composing and producing his lithographs.

[1] Not a soft-ground etching as is stated by Groschwitz, *op. cit.,* Check List No. 7.

PLATE 52
L'HOTEL DE SENS, PARIS

Chromolithograph, $14\frac{3}{4} \times 10\frac{3}{4}$ ins/375×273 mm.
Signed (On wall at L) T. Boys
Inscribed (BL) HOTEL DE SENS, PARIS
Plate XIV in *Picturesque Architecture in Paris, Ghent, Antwerp, Rouen etc.,* London, 1839.
Photograph by Lauros-Giraudon.

PLATE 52A (above)
L'HOTEL DE SENS, PARIS

Red chalk and pencil on tracing-paper, $14\frac{4}{5} \times 10\frac{11}{16}$ ins/376×272 mm. (pencil outlines).
British Museum, London (1952.5.10.15).
Reproduced by courtesy of the Trustees of the British Museum.

This tracing drawing and the chromolithograph are the final stages of the process begun in 1833 (Plate 49).
Boys produced a new version of the Hôtel for his 1839 Paris series. He did not wish the figure composition
to be identical to that in the 1835 lithograph (Plate 50), so he again worked out his new ideas on a tracing-
paper drawing. As in Plate 51 we see the successive superimposition of different ideas, some of which appear in the 1835 lithograph. In the final chromolithograph, Boys's definitive version of this subject,
the Hôtel is dignified and impressive, with its picturesque towers and eaves. The treatment has none of
the fussiness of the 1833 watercolour and is brighter and less grey in tone.

130

HOTEL DE SENS. PARIS

PLATE 53
THE PAVILLON DE FLORE, PARIS
Watercolour heightened with bodycolour and gum arabic, $17\frac{13}{16} \times 13$ ins/452 × 330 mm.
Fitzwilliam Museum, Cambridge.
Reproduced by permission of the Syndics of the Fitzwilliam Museum.

This version of the *Pavillon de Flore* is derived from the watercolour of 1829 (Frontispiece). The latter is rather faded but the Fitzwilliam picture retains all the brilliance of Boys's fresh colours. The scene is calm and delicate exhibiting the full mastery of composition which he had attained by this stage. This in turn looks back to a Bonington prototype in the Cecil Higgins Museum, Bedford, by way of a sketch sold at Christie's on 5 March, 1974 (lot 182, illustrated, see catalogue entry).

PLATE 54
THE PAVILLON DE FLORE, PARIS

Watercolour, $13\frac{3}{4} \times 10\frac{3}{8}$ ins/349 × 263 mm.
Henry E. Huntington Art Gallery, San Marino, California (59.55.120).

PLATE 55
THE PAVILLON DE FLORE, PARIS

Chromolithograph, $13\frac{1}{2} \times 11\frac{1}{2}$ ins/343 × 292 mm.
Signed (BC) T Boys
Inscribed (BR) PAVILLON DE FLORE TUILERIES
Plate XXI in *Picturesque Architecture in Paris, Ghent, Antwerp, Rouen etc.*, London, 1839.

Boys obviously decided early on that he would include a view of the Pavillon de Flore in his series on Paris. Having depicted it before (Plate 53) he wished to vary its format to be more faithful to the title of the series—*Picturesque Architecture*. The difference between the final chromolithograph and the earlier finished watercolours is that more of the Pavillon is shown, giving a different and more appropriate emphasis to the composition. He retains, by and large, the figures of his earlier versions, changing only the extent of the architecture. The sketch illustrated provides the link in this process. In it Boys has concentrated exclusively on sketching the larger expanse of the Pavillon. He already had the precise architectural details of the building and the figural composition, so it was unnecessary to draw them again. The sketch provides evidence that Boys used wash sketches as well as finished watercolours and outline drawings as preliminaries for his chromolithographs.

134

PLATE 56
HOTEL CLUNY, PARIS
Chromolithograph, $10\frac{3}{4} \times 13\frac{7}{8}$ ins/273×353 mm.
Signed (On flysheet on left gate pillar) T. BOYS/FARCEUR/No. I
Inscribed (BL) HOTEL DE CLUNY, PARIS
Plate XIII in *Picturesque Architecture in Paris, Ghent, Antwerp, Rouen etc.*, London, 1839.
Photograph by courtesy of the Albany Gallery, London.

This was one of the views produced by Boys as specimens for the inspection of reviewers prior to the actual publication of the series; the others included the *Court of the Hôtel de Cluny, St Laurent, Rouen* and *The Byloke, Ghent*. It is a most unusual composition with the imposing forms of the Hôtel dominating the narrow street. The shadow cast across the foreground wall provides an effective contrast to the brilliant sunlight on the stonework in the centre. The burst of vapoury blue in the sky above the architecture adds a final touch. The introduction of a note of self-parody in the inscription on the pillar is very characteristic.

An orange chalk on tracing-paper drawing, in which the figures differ from those in the final chromo-lithograph, is in a private collection in America.

136

PLATE 57
RUE NOTRE DAME, PARIS

Chromolithograph, $14\frac{1}{2} \times 10\frac{1}{2}$ ins/369 × 267 mm.
Signed (On bridle of left-hand horse) T B
Dated (On bridle of right-hand horse) 36
Inscribed (BL) NOTRE DAME. PARIS.
Plate XVIII in *Picturesque Architecture in Paris, Ghent, Antwerp, Rouen, etc.*, London, 1839.
Photograph by courtesy of the Albany Gallery, London.

La Rue Neuve Notre Dame, where Boys stood for this view, is no longer in existence, so this picture is of special interest as a portrayal of part of the irretrievable past. Boys was fascinated by the shops, which take up the greater part of this lithograph. He delights in the rows of old boots with their price tags, the varied shop signs, the horses and carts. Notre Dame itself looms in the background almost as an auxiliary feature. It is the street life, the perspective of buildings contrasted with bare expanses of stone which form the main subject matter. The colour composition is cool and restrained with soft browns, reds and blues forming delicate and subtle harmonies. Boys displays here a confidence and mastery which belie the fact that the work forms part of the first chromolithographic series of views ever issued.

The British Museum possesses a red chalk and pencil tracing-paper drawing for this view ($14\frac{1}{4} \times 10\frac{1}{2}$ ins/ 362 × 267 mm., 1952.5.10.6). The architecture is traced but the figures are obviously improvised. A private collector in America possesses another tracing drawing made as a preparatory sketch for the chromolithograph. It is interesting also to compare this view with that in Plate 20, which is taken much closer to Notre Dame.

NOTRE DAME. PARIS

PLATE 58
THE INSTITUTE, PARIS

Chromolithograph, $16\frac{1}{8} \times 11\frac{1}{2}$ ins/410 × 292 mm.
Signed (BL) T Boys 1839.
Inscribed (BR) LA CHAPELLE DE L'INSTITUT, PARIS.
Plate XXIII in *Picturesque Architecture in Paris, Ghent, Antwerp, Rouen etc.*, London, 1839.
Photograph by courtesy of the Albany Gallery, London.

This view shows a marvellous golden sunset bathing the whole scene in warmth. A favourite building of Boys, which he painted in several different watercolours (Plate 15), is here given an entirely new interpretation. The touches of red and blue in the figures give appropriate accents, and provide a diagonal stretching away towards the distance in contrast to the predominant verticals of the building.

PLATE 59
ST ETIENNE DU MONT, WITH THE PANTHEON, PARIS

Chromolithograph, $13\frac{7}{8} \times 11\frac{3}{8}$ ins/353 × 289 mm.
Inscribed (BR) ST ETIENNE DU MONT AND THE PANTHEON, PARIS.
Plate XX in *Picturesque Architecture in Paris, Ghent, Antwerp, Rouen, etc.*, London, 1839.
Photograph by courtesy of the Albany Gallery, London.

The only night scene in the series, and indeed in Boys's entire *oeuvre,* this daring concept has succeeded in every way. In his 'Descriptive Notice', Boys said that he aimed at 'variety in the aspects of nature', and describes this view as one of 'pale moonlight'. The wide-open expanse of this view, with its diminutive foreground figures, helps to intensify the atmosphere and reveals a romantic side to Boys's work.

The British Museum has a tracing-paper drawing for the lithograph ($13\frac{7}{8} \times 11\frac{15}{16}$ ins/353 × 296 mm., 1952.5.10.8). The architecture is traced, the figures are sketched in, and Boys has changed the position of the moon, an indication of the care he took over his composition.

142

PLATE 60
NOTRE DAME, PARIS

Chromolithograph, $9\frac{7}{8} \times 15\frac{1}{8}$ ins/248 × 384 mm.
Signed (BC) T Boys
Inscribed (BL) NOTRE DAME, PARIS FROM THE QUAI ST. BERNARD
Plate XXIV in *Picturesque Architecture in Paris, Ghent, Antwerp, Rouen etc.*, London, 1839.
Photograph by courtesy of the Albany Gallery, London.

Without doubt this chromolithograph is one of the finest ever produced: the colours are balanced, the drawing precise and delicate, the tones carefully worked and disposed. The composition has an almost inevitable feel about it: the low barrels in the foreground, the vertical white buildings on the *quai* and the low grey form of the Notre Dame. The subtle gradations of the tints on the buildings and ground are beautifully heightened by the solid blues and whites of the sky.

An orange chalk on tracing-paper drawing for this view is in a private collection in America. An undated watercolour of *The Notre Dame from the Quai* (6 × 8 ins/152 × 203 mm., Private Collection in England), taken from nearer to the Cathedral and without the buildings at the left, shows a very different scene with Parisian figures under parasols filling out the foreground.

144

PLATE 61

MUSEUM STREET AND LITTLE BLAKE STREET, YORK

Pen and wash, 12 × 9 ins/305 × 228 mm.
York City Art Gallery (EC/WD 57).

PLATE 62

BOOTHAM AND BOOTHAM BAR, YORK

Pencil and wash, $8\frac{7}{8}$ × 12 ins/225 × 305 mm.
York City Art Gallery (EC/WD 96).

In 1841 *A Series of Views in York* with tinted lithographs by Boys was issued in York. The views were purely of local significance and seem to have been commissioned as early as 1837 (Plate 1, *St Helen's Square and Stonegate,* is signed and dated). These two drawings do not relate directly to the lithographs but were obviously part of the series of preparatory drawings made for the series. Different in character to the tracing-paper drawings for the London and Paris series they have more body—indicated by the sparse use of thin washes. They still have the architectural precision but are invested with an atmosphere beyond that of a bare tracing drawing. The figures and the rather mannered coaches and horses were sketched in after the architecture had been drawn, but do not knit together to form a cohesive composition.

146

PLATE 63
THE STRAND

Lithograph, $16\frac{3}{8} \times 12\frac{5}{16}$ ins/416×313 mm.
Signed (On cart) T. S. BOYS/90 Gt. PORT. A.
Inscribed (BL) THE STRAND
Outline proof for Plate XXI in *London as it is,* London, 1842.
Guildhall Library, City of London.

PLATE 64
THE STRAND

Lithotint, $16\frac{3}{8} \times 12\frac{5}{16}$ ins/416×313 mm.
Tint proof for Plate XXI in *London as it is,* London, 1842.
Guildhall Library, City of London.

Both these proofs are preserved in the book of Tints and Outlines for the London series in the Guildhall Library.[1] The book contains an outline and a tint proof for each lithograph in the London series. (Sometimes Boys experimented with a second tint stone to achieve a more successful variation.)

The outline proof is skilfully drawn using line and cross-hatching to build up form and texture. It is a simple drawing. The tint proof has the masses of the forms brushed in, giving body to the whole. The same precise outline is kept, but there is no attempt to draw lines with lithotint; it is just washed in to fill in the outlines. The clouds of the sky are briefly sketched in, having been left out in the outline proof, Boys apparently implying that clouds cannot be drawn with lines.

[1] The book of progressive proofs for the Paris series is in a private collection in the USA. It contains the separate proofs of each colour used in each plate, and shows the tremendous care and judgment needed in the creation of a chromolithograph.

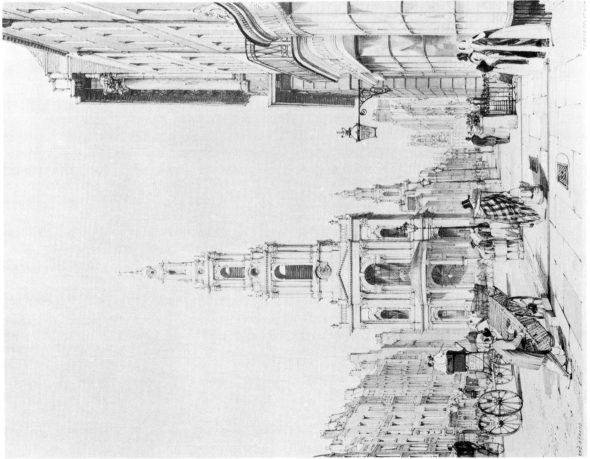

PLATE 65
THE STRAND
Hand-coloured tinted lithograph, $16\frac{3}{5} \times 12\frac{5}{16}$ ins/422×313 mm.
Signed (On cart) T.S. BOYS/90 Gt. PORT. A.
Inscribed (BL) THE STRAND
(UR) T.S. BOYS DEL ET LITH.
Plate XXI in *London as it is,* London, 1842.
Guildhall Library, City of London.

By combining the outline and tint proofs illustrated on the previous page, Boys obtained the final mono-chrome lithograph. The colouring is simply an embellishment, possibly added for commercial reasons, coloured versions being more saleable. The hand-colouring is delicate and thin, adding the barest tints to the underlying lithograph. The qualities of the lithograph are enhanced rather than obscured, so it was not really a contradiction of the principles of the series, namely to produce a work in monochrome lithography which could stand up on its own merits as a series of lithographs, rather than be seen as imitations of watercolours.

150

PLATE 66
HYDE PARK, NEAR GROSVENOR GATE
Hand-coloured tinted lithograph, $9\frac{5}{8} \times 18\frac{1}{4}$ ins/245 × 463 mm.
Inscribed (BL) HYDE PARK, NEAR GROSVENOR GATE
(UR) T.S. BOYS DEL ET LITHOG
Plate XVI in *London as it is,* London, 1842.
Guildhall Library, City of London.

'The view of Hyde Park is a good one, and gives a good idea of the crowds of company who delight therein to promenade, or "show" on horseback and in elegant equipages'.[1] This lithograph forms a fashion plate of London society in 1842, exquisite in conception, design and execution. It compares in feeling and delicacy of touch with the *Boulevard des Italiens, Paris* (Plate 28) which Boys painted some nine years earlier in Paris.

[1] Supplement to *The Times,* 1842. Extract preserved in the Guildhall Library, London.

PLATE 67
ST DUNSTAN'S &c. FLEET STREET
Hand-coloured tinted lithograph, $16\frac{7}{8} \times 12\frac{3}{8}$ ins/429 × 314 mm.
Signed (On cart in centre) T.S. BOYS/GOODS REMOVED/TOWN-COUNTRY.
Inscribed (BR) ST DUNSTANS &c. FLEET STREET
      (UL) T.S. BOYS DEL ET LITH
Plate XXIII in *London as it is,* London, 1842.
Guildhall Library, City of London.

'The view of the western and eastern approaches to Temple Bar, viz, the Strand and Fleet Street, close to that venerable edifice, are not only very perfect as mere representations of the houses and buildings in the neighbourhood, and entitled to great praise as architectural drawings, but there are a spirit and a life in the scenes which tell the spectator at once what sort of places they are, what is continually being done in their locality, and what is the state of the trade and traffic therein carried on, almost without intermission. In the picture, as in the reality, this part of London as it is seems almost impassable for foot passengers and somewhat dangerous for those in carriages, such wedging, jambing, crowding, jostling and so forth, that it is almost miraculous that each passenger threads his way through the throng, and that so few accidents occur to life and limb.'[1]

[1] Supplement to *The Times,* 1842. Extract preserved in the Guildhall Library, London.

154

PLATE 68
THE HORSEGUARDS &c. FROM ST JAMES'S PARK
Hand-coloured tinted lithograph, $9\frac{5}{8} \times 17\frac{3}{4}$ ins/245 × 451 mm.
Inscribed (BL) THE HORSE GUARDS &c. FROM ST JAMES'S PARK
(UR) T. SHOTTER BOYS DEL ET LITH
Plate XIV in *London as it is,* London, 1842.
Guildhall Library, City of London.

'In those representations of portions of the metropolis which are most strictly pictorial, and in which the artist may, without infringing the truth of representation, indulge in the beauties of the landscape—that is the views of St James's Park—he has produced very beautiful pictures. These views, at the same time that they delineate with accuracy and convey a perfect notion of the places themselves, form very delightful representations of the foliage of trees, the herbage and grass, and the natural scenery of the *rura in urbe,* in which, unfortunately, great towns do not sufficiently abound, but of which London as it is has, perhaps, its share, when it is considered how precious land is for building and with what difficulty the pressure of population is restrained from the occupancy of every untenanted spot in the metropolis.'[1]

[1] Supplement to *The Times,* 1842. Extract preserved in the Guildhall Library, London.

PLATE 69
REGENT STREET, LOOKING TOWARDS THE DUKE OF YORK'S COLUMN

Hand-coloured tinted lithograph, $12\frac{3}{8} \times 16\frac{3}{4}$ ins/315 × 425 mm.
Inscribed (BL)   REGENT STREET, LOOKING TOWARDS THE DUKE OF YORK'S COLUMN
        (UR) T.S. BOYS DEL ET LITHOG.
Plate XIX in *London as it is,* London, 1842.
Guildhall Library, City of London.

'The bustle and animation of this part of the town is graphic and characteristic. The turmoil of business and pleasure, the cares, exigencies, and varieties of fashion and labour, are all set forth in the groups of pedestrians and equestrians, in the carriages of the rich and noble, and the wains and waggons of the industrious and humble; carts, chariots, cabs, omnibuses, drays, all mingle in the noisy crowd, and concur in carrying out the design of the artist, and showing both life and London as they are. As pictures, these are well got up, the outline is correct, and the details made to assist the general effect.'[1]

[1] Supplement to *The Times,* 1842. Extract preserved in the Guildhall Library, London.

158

PLATE 70
THE CLUB-HOUSES, PALL MALL
Hand-coloured tinted lithograph, $12\frac{3}{8} \times 17\frac{5}{8}$ ins/314×447 mm.
Inscribed (BL) THE CLUB-HOUSES &c. PALL MALL
       (UR) T. SHOTTER BOYS DEL ET LITH.
Plate XIII in *London as it is*, London, 1842.
Guildhall Library, City of London.

This view has remained almost unchanged up to the present day. The Club Houses still exist, although the elegant carriages awaiting their owners are now gone forever, replaced by modern cars and taxis. As usual, Boys has introduced a piece of street genre, with the workmen putting up scaffolding on the left, strangely out of place in the fashionable and genteel life of Pall Mall.

160

PLATE 71
MANSION HOUSE, CHEAPSIDE, &c.
Hand-coloured tinted lithograph, $12\frac{1}{2} \times 16\frac{7}{8}$ ins/ 317 × 429 mm.
Signed (On shop board in background) T S BOYS/PAINTER
Inscribed (BL) MANSION HOUSE, CHEAPSIDE &c.
        (UR) T. SHOTTER BOYS DEL ET LITH.
Plate II in *London as it is,* London, 1842.
Guildhall Library, City of London.

'It would be endless to specify what the good taste of most persons will at once discover: there is in the execution of the work scarcely anything to find fault with, and the public, not only of this country, but of the continent, are greatly indebted to Mr T. S. Boys, the artist, by whom the original drawings and lithographs have been made, and also to his relation, Mr H.[1] Boys, of Golden Square, the publisher, for the manner in which the whole has been got up and introduced to them. The work is worth general, we may say, universal patronage: it ought to be in the possession of every native of Great Britain who can afford to purchase it, as a matter of national history and instruction, and every foreigner who can afford to give the comparatively moderate price charged for it,[2] should procure a copy that he may form a correct notion of a city with which every inhabitant of the civilized world is, in some degree or other, connected and interested.'[3]

[1] This should be 'T.' not 'H.'
[2] Bound they cost only £4.4s. in sepia monochrome, and £10.10s. coloured by hand and mounted in a portfolio. Separate impressions cost 4s. each in monochrome, 7s. 6d. coloured, and 10s. coloured and mounted.
[3] Supplement to *The Times,* 1842. Extract preserved in the Guildhall Library, London.

PLATE 72
THE RACE COURSE, SHREWSBURY

Watercolour, $7\frac{1}{8} \times 10\frac{5}{8}$ ins/181 × 270 mm.
Inscribed (BL) The White Hall from the Grandstand. 1842.
Private Collection, England.
Photograph by courtesy of the Manning Gallery, London.

This watercolour shows Boys's new-found freedom at the beginning of the 1840s. Made on a visit to the Midlands, it is sketched in broad sweeps of the brush. Very wet washes are employed almost exclusively, with little use of Boys's usual dragged granular colour. The one embellishment is the scratching on the foliage and posts round the course to give emphasis to them. This attractive, fresh watercolour conveys a feeling of space and atmosphere.

164

PLATE 73
ST PAUL'S FROM LAMBETH

Sepia wash, 4 × 8 ins/102 × 203 mm.
Inscribed (Verso) St. Pauls from Lambeth 1844
Private Collection, England.
Photograph by courtesy of the Manning Gallery, London.

This small sepia sketch shows clearly a side of Boys's watercolour technique that came to the fore during the 1840s. The sketch, treated very briefly and atmospherically, conveys by means of mass the buildings and landmarks of London. Boys skilfully employed wet washes to form the storm clouds in the sky, and dragged washes to create the water of the Thames. He relied purely on sepia applied with a brush, there being no drawing to give details of the architecture.

PLATE 74
DURHAM

Watercolour, $3\frac{1}{2} \times 7\frac{1}{4}$ ins/89 × 184 mm.
Collection unknown.

PLATE 75
DURHAM CATHEDRAL

Watercolour, $10\frac{1}{2} \times 13\frac{1}{2}$ ins/267 × 343 mm.
Collection unknown.
Photographs by courtesy of the Fine Art Society, London.

The small sketch shows some features in common with Plates 77 and 78 in its broad treatment of the masses and the horizontal bands of wet washes in the sky. It is, however, a more meticulous work with greater attention paid to detail and the use of knife scratches to give lights to the river. The large watercolour (which was possibly the one exhibited at the New Water-colour Society in 1845) further develops the techniques used in the sketch. Scratching out is used in the water and the foreground features. The overall treatment is dry and precise, emphasizing the rising towers of the Cathedral and the dark wooded cliffs over the river. This type of treatment harks back to his York view of ten years earlier (Plate 38) and shows a certain maturity, very different from the youthful sparkle of his French watercolours of the 1830s.

PLATE 76
LA TOUR DE BEFFROI, CALAIS

Lithotint, $14\frac{1}{16} \times 9\frac{7}{8}$ ins/357 × 251 mm.
Signed (On shop board at R) T.S. BOYS
Inscribed (UL) <u>T.S. Boys lithotint</u>
         (UR) <u>Procédé Hullmandel</u>
         (UC) <u>La Tour de Beffroi, Calais/Picardie</u>
Plate in *Voyages Pittoresques; Picardie,* Vol. III, Paris, 1845.
Reproduced from the copy in the University Library, Cambridge.

This lithograph is rendered purely with the use of lithotint, unsupported by a drawing stone. All the lines and tones are sketched in with a brush. Possibly the even tone of the sky was achieved with the aid of the stump. Though a little insubstantial, it is brilliantly executed, revealing Boys's capacity for this difficult technique. The scene has a lightness and gaiety that would not have been possible had he used any other method. This was Boys's last contribution to the *Voyages Pittoresques,* which he had enriched over the years with his high-quality lithographs.

170

PLATE 77
LANDSCAPE WITH MILL IN THE DISTANCE

Watercolour, $3\frac{7}{8} \times 6\frac{3}{8}$ ins/98 × 162 mm.
Private Collection, England.

PLATE 78
SHIPPING OFF THE COAST

Watercolour, $4\frac{3}{4} \times 7$ ins/121 × 178 mm.
Private Collection, England.
Photographs by courtesy of the Manning Gallery, London.

These two watercolour sketches exemplify Boys's free handling of his sketches in the mid-1840s. They have the same loose control that was present in *St Paul's from Lambeth* (Plate 73). The colours are fresh, but not bright, and are washed on in broad, wet brushstrokes. In the sky he has daubed colour on top of a still-damp underwash in order to obtain the effect of clouds. The forms are briefly sketched with little use of pencil-work underneath. The total effect is light and atmospheric, displaying the artist's keen delight in painting the everyday aspects of nature.

PLATE 79
AT CHELTENHAM
Watercolour heightened with bodycolour, $18\frac{3}{4} \times 10\frac{3}{8}$ ins/476 × 263 mm.
Cheltenham Art Gallery and Museum.

This watercolour, exhibited at the New Water-colour Society (see Appendix B), shows Boys looking back to such pictures as the *Boulevard des Italiens* (Plate 28) and *Hyde Park, near Grosvenor Gate* (Plate 66). As in these two works, he portrays a scene with fashionable ladies and gentlemen promenading down the street. These were the very same people whom Boys had come to teach in Cheltenham in 1846 (see Chapter 5, page 55). The bold treatment of the trees with their russet colours and the brilliant bursts of blue in the sky recall the works of his youth. However, the buildings and figures do not have the variety and individual characterization of his Paris view. The composition is most unusual, framing the Cathedral between the upward surges of the trees lining the avenue (the Old Well Walk). From his letter Boys was obviously in a depressed state of mind while he was in Cheltenham, but this scene seems to have inspired him to cast off his gloom and produce a work of rare quality.

PLATE 80
STREET SCENE AT STRATFORD BY BOW

Watercolour, $4\frac{3}{4} \times 8\frac{1}{4}$ ins/121 $\times$ 210 mm.
Collection of Mr and Mrs Paul Mellon.

PLATE 81
STORM ON THE COAST

Watercolour, pen and ink, $5\frac{1}{4} \times 7\frac{3}{8}$ ins/133 $\times$ 187 mm.
Collection of Mr and Mrs Paul Mellon.

These two watercolours are related to each other by the dramatic and powerful washes of paint. In the *Street Scene* the long dark shadow stretches across the road and, with the menacing clouds, threatens a coming storm. Such a storm is rendered with an almost violent use of washes in the other work. The flat and plain stretch of sand is assaulted by the dark masses of the sky and the lashing squalls of rain. The scratched out whites of the seagulls are the only living forms in this forlorn and devastated scene.

The unfinished *Street Scene* shows the mechanics by which Boys built up his picture. The feint outline pencil drawing, perhaps traced on (as suggested by the pin-holes in the corners) is overlaid with broad washes which in their turn are shadowed with different shades of their own colour, and rubbed and worked. Finally, he has picked out the pencil details with ink. The use of pen and ink is unusual for Boys as he was accustomed to using sepia brushwork to render his architectural details.

176

PLATE 82
CANAL IN A CONTINENTAL TOWN
Watercolour, 8 × 10⅜ ins/203 × 264 mm.
Signed (BC, on wall) <u>Boys</u>
With the Albany Gallery, London, 1974.
Photograph by courtesy of the Albany Gallery.

This watercolour is difficult to assign to any particular period of Boys's career. The style is mature and economical, with its skilful build-up of oranges and blues to form harmonies rather than contrasts. This type of picturesquely crumbling architecture constantly fascinated Boys because of its uneven lines, forms and shadows. The figures, sketched in with the lightest of touches, are fairly similar to those in the boat in the *St Paul's from Lambeth* (Plate 73) but the rest of the treatment is altogether more subtle than the rather primitive massings of forms in that sketch. Perhaps a date towards the end of the 1840s is the most satisfactory. The range of colours and the subtle contrasts of long shadows against the white facades of the houses display a confidence lacking in his works of the early 1840s.

178

PLATE 83
AMIENS ON THE SOMME

Watercolour, $29\frac{3}{8} \times 40\frac{5}{8}$ ins/746 × 1032 mm.
Signed (BL) Thos Boys./1849.
Walker Art Gallery, Liverpool.

Exhibited at the New Water-colour Society in 1849 and at the International Exhibition in 1862,[1] this watercolour was one of the most important that Boys painted in the latter part of his life. Boys certainly thought so or he would not, in 1862, have recalled a watercolour painted some thirteen years previously to be his showpiece in such an important exhibition. Carefully and correctly treated, it lacks the qualities of his earlier watercolours and of the light and free sketches that he was painting contemporaneously. Its large scale was unsuited to his watercolour style as a whole. Looking back to his earlier style of the 1830s, it is certainly an admirable picture, if only in scale and execution. Boys would have regarded it as being in competition with large finished oil paintings. It was the current vogue at this time to work up watercolours to look like oils and to give them heavy gilt frames. Unfortunately, this conception led to the death of spontaneity, freedom and purity in watercolour painting.

[1] See Appendix B.

180

Plate 84 is similar in format to the etchings by Boys after Ruskin's drawings in *Examples of the Architecture of Venice,* by John Ruskin, London, 1851, for which it was presumably intended. The etching is very fine, showing a brilliant control of the effects of sunlight on masonry. Boys manages to achieve a very real feel for the volumes of the architecture, as distinct from pure detail.

The Bar-Gate, Southampton is unique in Boys's work because of its apparent mannerisms. He has over-drawn with pen and ink the details of the architecture and the forms of the figures, carts and other accessories. The treatment of the horses and the people is very characteristic and recalls that in his earlier York views (Plates 61 and 62). The odd mixture of pen and watercolour gives this work its decidedly archaic and quaint atmosphere.

PLATE 86
WALMER CASTLE, LOOKING EAST TOWARDS DEAL

Watercolour, $3\frac{3}{4} \times 14\frac{3}{8}$ ins/95 × 365 mm.
Private Collection, England (formerly in the possession of Spink and Son Ltd.).

PLATE 87
THE DUKE OF WELLINGTON'S CHAMBER, WALMER CASTLE

Watercolour, $10\frac{3}{8} \times 14\frac{3}{8}$ ins/264 × 365 mm.
Inscribed (BR) The Duke's Chamber/Sketched at Walmer Castle.
Collection of Mr and Mrs Paul Mellon.

At the beginning of the 1850s Boys was commissioned to make sketches of Apsley House and Walmer Castle, the homes of the late Duke of Wellington, to be lithographed in a commemorative volume. Two of these lithographs are illustrated here (Plates 88 and 89). On one of his visits to Walmer Castle Boys dashed off the little sketch with the characteristic loose treatment which we find in his work of this later period. Contrasting with this is the painting of the Duke's chamber, with its formal composition. This was lithographed exactly as Plate X in the Apsley House series (Plate 89). The Victorian air of the sketch is produced by the subject matter rather than by Boys's treatment.

184

PLATE 88
THE STRIPED DINING ROOM, APSLEY HOUSE
Hand-coloured lithograph, $10\frac{7}{16} \times 14\frac{7}{16}$ ins/265 × 367 mm.
Plate III in *Apsley House and Walmer Castle,* London, 1853.
Victoria and Albert Museum, London.
Photograph by courtesy of the Victoria and Albert Museum.

PLATE 89
**THE ROOM IN WHICH THE DUKE OF WELLINGTON DIED,
WALMER CASTLE**
Hand-coloured lithograph, $10\frac{1}{4} \times 14\frac{5}{16}$ ins/260 × 363 mm.
Plate X in *Apsley House and Walmer Castle,* London, 1853.
Victoria and Albert Museum, London.
Photograph by courtesy of the Victoria and Albert Museum.

These lithographs were executed after Boys's watercolours by the employees of Messrs Hanhart Ltd. It is they who are responsible for the gaudy and Victorian character of the hand-colouring. The actual drawing, however, is well done and carries out perfectly the details of Boys's own preparatory watercolours (*e.g.* Plate 87). These lithographs can hardly have done Boys's reputation any good, as they are sadly inferior productions, unworthy of his name.

186

PLATE 90
COWLEY MANOR: THE SOUTH FRONT
Watercolour heightened with bodycolour, $10\frac{3}{4} \times 7\frac{1}{4}$ ins/273×184 mm.
Private Collection, England.

As discussed in the text (page 57) this watercolour is probably an idealized architectural realization of George Somers Clarke's designs for Cowley Manor in Gloucestershire, remodelled for James Hutchinson after 1852. This watercolour was originally part of a large panorama of the Manor, but it was cut up and several sections are now lost. The colouring is subtle and understated, and there is a clever variation of intensity along the different sections of the walls. In his usual manner, Boys has touched in figures with bright and vivid blues, reds, greens and whites. In the foreground the dry scumbling of white bodycolour over the beige of the background walls to represent a fountain is particularly effective, and unusual in Boys's *oeuvre*.

PLATE 91
LODGE IN A PARK
Watercolour heightened with bodycolour, $9\frac{1}{2} \times 10\frac{3}{4}$ ins/241 × 273 mm.
Private Collection, England.

Stylistically this watercolour, though not part of the original panorama of Cowley Manor, must be related to it. As far as can be ascertained this cottage no longer exists. It is possible, however, that this little piece of Gothic extravagance was never built, but was only realized in Boys's watercolour. In support of this idea, one can see that the pencil lines of the roof and chimney extend beyond their limits, as in an architectural elevation. The treatment is the same as that in the *Cowley Manor: the South Front* (Plate 90). The handling of the trees is free and impressionistic in its use of varying shades of green and different types of brushwork.

190

PLATE 92
FRIAR STREET, WORCESTER

Watercolour, $13\frac{3}{4} \times 20\frac{1}{8}$ ins/350 × 510 mm.
Signed (BC) Friar Street Worcester. Thos. Boys./1859.
Worcester District Museum and Art Gallery.
Photograph by courtesy of Frank T. Sabin Ltd., London.

PLATE 93
MARKET HALL, SHREWSBURY

Watercolour, $13\frac{7}{8} \times 20\frac{1}{8}$ ins/352 × 510 mm.
Signed (BR) Thos. Boys Shrewsbury.
Shrewsbury District Museums.
Photograph by courtesy of Shrewsbury District Museums.

Both these watercolours were exhibited at the New Water-colour Society Exhibition in 1860 (see Appendix B). They formed part of a new project by Boys to produce a large series of works, possibly to be engraved in a proposed publication entitled *Remains of Old England,* to follow up his Paris and London series. It is unlikely that this series would have had the appeal of the earlier ones as they lack their sparkling lines and imaginative compositions. However, they do have a charm, and neither Shrewsbury nor Worcester ever claimed to be the busy centres and fashionable *rendezvous* that London and Paris were. This type of architecture obviously delighted Boys and he renders its irregularities with care and admiration, unlike most of the artists of his day who preferred to ignore it completely.

PLATE 94
THE VALE OF LLANGOLLEN
Watercolour, $9\frac{13}{16} \times 17\frac{7}{8}$ ins/249 × 454 mm.
Inscribed (Verso) The Vale of Llangollen
Victoria and Albert Museum, London (P28–1930).
Crown copyright reserved.

This sketch was probably painted on one of Boys's sketching tours through Wales in the early 1860s. The brief, impressionistic rendering of the open Welsh countryside suggests that it was painted on the spot. The only colours employed are yellows, browns and greens, which are deployed to create a whole range of relationships of tone and texture. The use of bare paper is interesting and effective as a contrast to the coloured washes. Considering the youthful freedom of this sketch it is hard to believe that at the same time the artist was producing such tired and overworked watercolours as those shown in Plates 98 and 99.

194

PLATE 95
BAMBOROUGH CASTLE

Watercolour, $4\frac{7}{8} \times 13\frac{3}{4}$ ins/124×349 mm.
Private Collection, England.

This watercolour is undated but it was probably painted towards the end of Boys's life. It relates most closely to the pictures and sketches he made of Wales during the early 1860s. The control of the washes is echoed in the view of *Nant ffrancon*[1] sketched on one of the Welsh tours. The light and fresh colours with their sandy yellow and warm browns show that it was painted *en plein air*. Unfortunately, there appear to be no other watercolours depicting this part of England painted by Boys in his later years.

[1] Watercolour, $4\frac{7}{8} \times 8\frac{5}{8}$ ins/124×219 mm., signed <u>T.S. BOYS</u>; Private Collection, England.

196

WATERGATE STREET, CHESTER

Watercolour heightened with bodycolour, $11\frac{5}{8} \times 8\frac{1}{2}$ ins/295 × 216 mm.
Signed (On shop sign, C) T.S. BOYS PAINTER
Inscribed (BL) WATERGATE ST. CHESTER/1862
Grosvenor Museum, Chester (44.A.61).

Painted for exhibition at the New Water-colour Society, this picture contrasts in style to Boys's large watercolours of Continental towns. It has a freedom, lightness and daring which are not present in watercolours such as those of Prague (Plates 97 and 98). Boys has created a feeling of depth in a masterly way, by alternate bands of sunlight and shadow stretching down the Row. The iridescent touches of green, red, orange and white set off the predominantly brown tones of the masonry and woodwork.

PLATE 97
PRAGUE

Watercolour, $15\frac{1}{4} \times 10\frac{7}{8}$ ins/387×276 mm.
Signed (BR) <u>Thos Boys.</u>
Collection of Mr and Mrs Paul Mellon.

This is one of a number of views of Continental towns which Boys exhibited at the New Water-colour Society during the latter part of his life. It varies from the others in that it is not concerned with a street or market scene; it has a more tranquil air. He has used techniques such as scratching out on the water and in the figures. The composition is carefully devised with its projecting forms in the foreground leading through towards, and complementing, the impressive spires of the town. These late Continental views were probably all done in his studio in England from drawings and sketches made during his earlier visits to his sister and brother-in-law in Darmstadt. It is not surprising then that they lack sparkle and adventure in the paintwork and colouring.

Thos Boys

PLATE 98
THE RATH HAUS AND THEIN KIRCHE, PRAGUE
Watercolour, $17 \times 13\frac{1}{4}$ ins/432×337 mm.
Signed (BR) RATH HAUS/THEIN KIRCHE/T.S. Boys/PRAGUE/1860.
Marc Fitch Fund.
Photograph by courtesy of the Fine Art Society, London.

PLATE 99
A VIEW IN LEIPZIG
Watercolour, $22 \times 16\frac{1}{4}$ ins/559×413 mm.
Signed (BC) Tho⁵ Boys./1857.
Private Collection, England.
Photograph by courtesy of The Fine Art Society, London.

These two watercolours illustrate the type of picture that Boys was exhibiting at the New Water-colour Society in the 1860s. They are large in size and impressive in composition, but they lack the *élan* and brilliance of his watercolours of the 1830s. In these works Boys was attempting to follow the then current trend in watercolours of competing with oil paintings in size and finish. Thus it compares closely to the work which Callow was doing at the same time and in particular to a view of the same square in Leipzig, taken from another angle. The general colouring of Boys's work of this date is rather tired pale blues and beiges with darker reds and browns in the figures; the feeling is very much that of watercolours worked up in the studio rather than executed *en plein air*.

PLATE 100
FOOTBRIDGE OVER A STREAM

Sepia wash over pencil, $13\frac{3}{8} \times 9\frac{7}{8}$ ins/340 × 251 mm.
Private Collection, England.
Purchased at the artist's sale, 30 Acacia Road, St John's Wood, London.

This type of drawing is difficult to date securely but it is probably later than the *Lodge* (Plate 91) in which the treatment of the foliage is similar, and before the free style of the late *Lake in a mountainous Landscape* (Plate 102). It was therefore probably painted during the 1860s. It is simply sepia wash over brief pencil outlines, and in it Boys exhibits complete control over his medium. He skilfully breaks up his sepia washes, allowing the white of the paper to play an important part as individual highlights. The overall feeling is relaxed and informal, befitting a simple experiment in tone composition of which he had shown himself to be the master from his earliest essays in painting.

PLATE 101
WASHERWOMAN AT THE WELL
Watercolour heightened with bodycolour and gum arabic, $12\frac{3}{4} \times 9$ ins/323×228 mm.
Private Collection, England.
Purchased at the artist's sale, 30 Acacia Road, St John's Wood, London.

Another of Boys's late sketches, this watercolour is notable for its freshness and its high-keyed colours. It is almost entirely in browns and oranges, apart from touches of green in the bushes and the red of the washerwoman's bag. The play of light on the masonry and the way in which the basin projects forward are highlights in this beautiful study. The washerwoman is wearing Continental dress, but it is possible that Boys executed this watercolour in England on one of his later sketching tours.

PLATE 102
LAKE IN A MOUNTAINOUS LANDSCAPE

Watercolour heightened with bodycolour and gum arabic, $10\frac{1}{4} \times 18\frac{3}{4}$ ins/261×476 mm.
Private Collection, England.
Purchased at the artist's sale, 30 Acacia Road, St John's Wood, London.

Standing apart in Boys's *oeuvre,* this watercolour has a dramatic intensity far removed from his usual style. It portrays a brilliant sunset with its myriad of contrasting colours and reflections. Boys has risen to the occasion in a masterly fashion, catching the true luminosity of such an evening. He has used every colour of the spectrum, working them together to create an overall warmth. In characteristic fashion he has placed little figures in a boat in the centre of the composition to give a focus. A touch of the bizarre is added by the figures under the trees in the foreground who appear to be climbing a ladder.

APPENDIX A
FAMILY HISTORY

Thomas Shotter Boys's forbears were descended ultimately from Ivo de Taillebois who came over to England with William the Conqueror.[1] The Taillebois family was given substantial properties in Holland and in different parts of the county of Lincolnshire: Welton le Marsh and Thorpe, near Wainfleet. The family lived at Welton, gradually changing their name from Taillebois through de Bosco, Bois, Boyce, until it finally became Boys. Boys's grandfather Thomas Boys was born at Welton in 1737. It was this Thomas Boys who effected the move from Lincolnshire to London; he died in 1801 at Golders Green, 'in Hendon'. From his will, dated 14 May 1800, it is obvious that the Boys family was still well-to-do. He held 'freehold estates in the counties of Southampton, Middlesex, Huntingdon, Lincolnshire and elsewhere', and copyhold estates in London. Possibly their assets were mostly in land as he did not leave especially substantial sums of money to his sons and daughters (of the thirteen children born to him, only four survived; of these James Boys—Shotter Boys's father—was the youngest). James Boys received £300 whereas his one elder brother and his eldest sister's husband received jointly all the freeholds and copyholds as well as the residue of Thomas Boys's personal property. Even taking into account the custom of primogeniture, it seems that James was unfairly treated. Perhaps he was out of favour with his father.

James Boys married Elizabeth Collins, who originally came from Bath, at Hendon on 28 October 1801. It is possible that his father had not allowed the marriage before his death; once he was dead they could proceed. James and Elizabeth lived most of their married life in White Lion Street, Pentonville, where James had bought a house. In his will he is described as a salesman by profession, but it is not known of what.[2] They had two children—Thomas Shotter and his sister Mary. James made his will in August 1805 after which date he made no further amendments. He died on 3 January 1821 leaving his house jointly to Thomas and Mary, and his money and effects to Elizabeth. His elder brother Thomas Boys, of Newgate Market, was one of the two guardians, indicating that the relationship between these two branches was close. Indeed, when Shotter Boys's guardian uncle died in June 1829, he left £250 to Elizabeth, £50 to Shotter Boys and a further £50 to the latter's sister, Mary. Boys's cousins were relatively well off as Thomas Boys, later to become a publisher of Shotter Boys's works, had received £1,000 before his father's death. It seems that the uneven distribution of wealth arranged by Shotter Boys's grandfather was having its effect in making this family rich and that of Shotter Boys relatively poor. Whereas Thomas Boys had been able to take up publishing with the aid of £1,000 from his father, Shotter Boys had had to go into apprenticeship under George Cooke, which had cost his father precisely £75.[3]

Shotter Boys remained on good terms with his cousin Thomas throughout his life. They both shared the same interest in art. It appears that Mary Boys was his favourite cousin, a further underlining of the close relationship between these branches of the family. Thomas married Caroline Rutter on 4 September 1823. Mary married William John Cooke, a nephew of George Cooke, on 13 November 1823 at St Augustin and St Faith, Watling Street. William John, born on 11 April 1797, was apparently in George Cooke's studio for a while and there could have met Shotter Boys and Mary, his future wife. He and Mary had one son, Montague William, who was born on 2 December 1824. In 1842 they went to live in Darmstadt,[4] remaining there until William John's death on 6 April 1867, after which Mary and Montague returned to England.

Shotter Boys married Célestine Marie Barbe (Barbe presumably being her maiden-name), who was Belgian and came from the town, or immediate vicinity, of Soignies. Boys must have met her on one of his visits to Belgium made during the late 1820s or early 1830s.[5] It is not known where or when they married. Célestine was some ten years younger than Shotter Boys[6] and it is probable that she would not have married before the age of twenty, which would have been about 1833. They were certainly married by 1846 as Boys refers to her in his letter written from Cheltenham.[7] They did not have any children so far as can be ascertained. Célestine survived her husband but it is not known where or when she died. No documents can be traced in England. She may have returned to Belgium, with the proceeds of her husband's studio sale, but again there is a lack of documents relating to her death or presence in Soignies after 1874.[8]

It is hoped that these details help to fill in the background and family relationships of Shotter Boys, which are important factors in his early youth and later unhappiness. Descendants of Thomas Boys, the publisher, have been traced, but it appears that they have no family documents which can add further information.

NOTES TO APPENDIX A

1 For further details of the Boys family history see *The Boys Family,* by Guy Ponsonby Boys, published in three volumes (British Museum, MS no. Add.44918): a valuable source for the documentary information contained in this Appendix.
2 Somerset House, London; will dated 16 August 1805.
3 The original indenture of apprenticeship is in the possession of C. R. Cooke, O.B.E.
4 Cooke, *op. cit.*
5 The following visits are attested by dated watercolours:
1830: *Hôtel de Bellevue and Café d'Amitié seen from the Park, Brussels* (Plate 14).
1832: *The Cathedral at Louvain,* watercolour, $10\frac{1}{2} \times 13\frac{3}{4}$ ins/266 × 349 mm., signed *T. Boys 1832* and inscribed *Boys Fripier* on a shop sign, Private Collection, England.
1835: *The Cathedral at Bruges,* watercolour, $11\frac{5}{8} \times 8\frac{1}{2}$ ins/295 × 216 mm., signed *Thos Boys/1835,* Birmingham City Art Gallery, by courtesy of Mrs Cecil Keith.
1836: *The Cathedral at Louvain,* watercolour, $12 \times 9\frac{3}{8}$ ins/305 × 238 mm., signed *Thos Boys/1836,* Private Collection, England.
6 Details from a census carried out in 1851 (from files in the Paul Mellon Centre for Studies in British Art) give Boys's age as 48, and his wife's as 38.
7 Letter cited.
8 Inquiries in Soignies have failed to uncover any material.

EXTRACT FROM THE BOYS FAMILY TREE

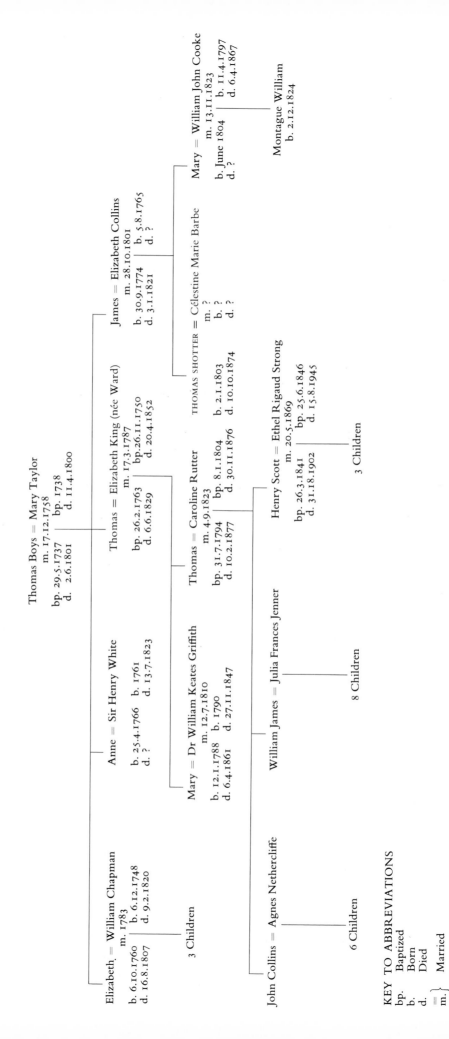

Thomas Boys = Mary Taylor
m. 17.12.1758
bp. 29.5.1737   bp. 1738
d.   2.6.1801   d. 11.4.1800

Elizabeth, = William Chapman
m. 1783
b. 6.10.1760   b. 6.12.1748
d. 16.8.1807   d. 9.2.1820

3 Children

Anne = Sir Henry White
m. 25.4.1766   b. 1761
b.   d. 13.7.1823
d. ?

Mary = Dr William Keates Griffith
m. 12.7.1810
b. 12.1.1788   b. 1790
d. 6.4.1861   d. 27.11.1847

John Collins = Agnes Nethercliffe

6 Children

Thomas = Elizabeth King (née Ward)
m. 17.3.1787
bp. 26.2.1763   bp. 26.11.1750
d. 6.6.1829   d. 20.4.1852

James = Elizabeth Collins
m. 28.10.1801
b. 30.9.1774   b. 5.8.1765
d. 3.1.1821   d. ?

Thomas = Caroline Rutter
m. 4.9.1823
bp. 31.7.1794   bp. 8.1.1804
d. 10.2.1877   d. 30.11.1876

THOMAS SHOTTER = Célestine Marie Barbe
b. 2.1.1803   m. ?
d. 10.10.1874   b. ?
                 d. ?

Mary = William John Cooke
m. 13.11.1823
b. June 1804   b. 11.4.1797
d. ?   d. 6.4.1867

Montague William
b. 2.12.1824

Henry Scott = Ethel Rigaud Strong
m. 20.5.1869
bp. 26.3.1841   bp. 25.6.1846
d. 31.18.1902   d. 15.8.1945

3 Children

William James = Julia Frances Jenner

8 Children

KEY TO ABBREVIATIONS
bp.   Baptized
b.   Born
d.   Died
=   } Married
m.   }

APPENDIX B
EXHIBITED WORKS

List of known works exhibited by Thomas Shotter Boys during his lifetime. (The address at the foot of each entry is that from which Boys submitted his work for exhibition.)

KEY TO ABBREVIATIONS
RA	Royal Academy
SBA	Society of British Artists, Suffolk Street
NWCS	New Water-colour Society
Salon	French Salon in Paris
Liverpool	Liverpool Society of Fine Arts
w/c	Watercolour or drawing
p	Oil painting

Year	Place and exhibition number	Title	Description
1824	SBA		
	563	*A Vase.*	w/c
1827	Salon		
	1207	*Une Tempête: d'après Vernet.*	engraving
	1577	*Vue du Temple de Phigalie.*	engraving
	1578	*Vue de l'île de Zéa et vase péruvien.*	engraving
		(15 Rue de la Rochefoucauld.)	
1829	SBA		
	509	*Hindoo Temple at Benares.*	w/c
	516	*Pierhead at Havre.*	w/c
	520	*Abbey of St Armand, Rouen.*	w/c
	526	*Scene on the Beach at Trouville, Normandy.*	w/c
		(34 Upper Seymour St., Euston Sq.)	
1830	SBA		
	390	*Coast Scene, Havre.*	p
	413	*Coast Scene, Normandy.*	p
	544	*Part of the Tuileries, and the Isle of the Cité, Paris.*	w/c
	730	*Horse Guards, St James's Park.*	w/c
		(44 Greek Street)	
1831	SBA		
	707	*Malines.*	w/c
	760	*La Chapelle à Mons.*	w/c
		(44 Greek Street.)	

Year	Place and exhibition number	Title	Description
1832	NWCS		
	247	*Nôtre Dame de Answick.*	w/c
	270	*King's Palace, Brussels.*	w/c
1833	Salon		
	272	*Cathedrale de Salisbury.*	w/c
	273	*Vue de Venise.*	w/c
	274	*La Rue Damiette, Rouen.*	w/c
	275	*Vue du Pont des Arts.*	w/c
	276	*L'Hôtel de Sens, à Paris.*	w/c?
	277	*La Rue Bailleul à Paris.*	w/c?
	278	*Anciennes maisons, à Chester.* (19 Rue du Bouloy.)	w/c?
1834	Salon		
	210	*Vue de l'Hôtel de Ville de Béthune.*	w/c
	211	*Vue de St Etienne du Mont à Paris.*	w/c
	212	*Vue de la Tour St Jacques la Boucherie.*	w/c
1835	Salon		
	244	*Vues de Paris.* (39 Rue du Mont-Blanc.)	w/c
	2374	*Temple de Phigalie.* (39 Rue de la Chaussée-d'Antin.)	engraving
	2464	*Fonts baptismaux de Morlaix (Finistière).* (*Voyage Pittoresque en Bretagne, par M. le comte de Trobriand*).	lithograph
1837	SBA		
	673	*Landscape.*	w/c
	739	*A view near Anderlecht.* (7 Albany Street.)	w/c
1838	SBA		
	569	*Greenwich, from the Observatory Hill.* (7 Albany Street, Regent's Park.)	p
1840	NWCS		
	65	*View in the Shambles, York.*	w/c
	129	*Rue de la Tuile, Rouen.* (7 Albany Street.)	w/c
1841	NWCS		
	69	*A Doorway to the Ancient College of Bayeux, Paris.*	w/c
	80	*A Doorway to the Madeleine, Paris.*	w/c
	257	*The Portes and Boulevards, St Denis and St Martin, Paris.*	w/c

214

	278	*The Conciergerie &c., Paris; scene from the Pont Neuf.* (7 Albany Street.)	w/c
1842	NWCS		
	169	*A Coast Scene.* (20 Howland Street, Fitzroy Sq.)	w/c
1843	NWCS		
	39	*Antwerp.*	w/c
	116	*At Prague.*	w/c
	197	*The Castle at Boulogne-sur-Mer.*	w/c
	256	*Part of the Wartburg, the retreat of Luther; from Russell's Tour in Germany, page 236.*	w/c
	287	*Abbeville.*	w/c
	330	*Dresden.*	w/c
	345	*Eisenach.*	w/c
	377	*Abbeville.* (81 Great Titchfield Street.)	w/c
1844	NWCS		
	113	*Dresden.*	w/c
	311	*Mentone, Coast of Genoa.*	w/c
	321	*In Boulogne Cathedral.* (81 Great Titchfield Street.)	w/c
1845	NWCS		
	89	*Highgate, from the Fields near Kentish Town.*	w/c
	167	*Entrance to Montreuil.*	w/c
	196	*At Trouville.*	w/c
	207	*The Beach at Folkestone.*	w/c
	303	*Durham.* (81 Great Titchfield Street.)	w/c
1846	NWCS		
	69	*Dresden.*	w/c
	77	*Paris—Gallery of the Louvre, seen from the Pont des Arts.*	w/c
	221	*Rue des Changes, Abbeville.*	w/c
	222	*At Marquise, near Boulogne.*	w/c
	247	*Fontaine de la Crosse, Rouen.* (81 Great Titchfield Street.)	w/c
1847	RA		
	558	*Rue de la Tuile, Rouen.* (81 Great Titchfield Street.)	p
	NWCS		
	57	*Bridge of Eltham Palace, Kent.*	w/c
	89	*At Cheltenham.*	w/c
	255	*Prague.*	w/c

Year	Place and exhibition number	Title	Description	Price £ s d
	267	*Tewkesbury Abbey, Worcestershire.* (81 Great Titchfield Street.	w/c	
1848	RA			
	1107	*Prague.* (81 Great Titchfield Street.)	p	
	NWCS			
	18	*At Beauvais.*	w/c	
	215	*Entry to the Cathedral yard, Gloucester.* (81 Great Titchfield Street.)	w/c	
1849	NWCS			
	87	*Windsor from Eton playing fields.*	w/c	
	91	*Paris, from near the Pont de Grenelle.*	w/c	
	116	*Windsor, from the Brocas Meadow.*	w/c	
	125	*Amiens, seen from the Banks of the Somme* (and passage about the magnificence of the Cathedral).	w/c	
	137	*Salisbury, looking towards the poultry market.*	w/c	
	240	*Hôtel de Ville, St Omer.*	w/c	
	347	*Facade of the ancient Bailiwick at Amiens. Temp. 1540.* (81 Great Titchfield Street.)	w/c	
1850	NWCS			
	22	*The Chapel of Edward the Confessor, Westminster Abbey: shewing the Shrine of Edward the Confessor, the Tomb and Chantry of Henry V and the Tomb of Henry III, builder of this part of the Abbey,* (and poem, Howlett's 'Westminster Abbey').	w/c	
	201	*Windsor. Sketch from nature.* (81 Great Titchfield Street.)	w/c	
1851	NWCS			
	25	*Venice–Tower of St Georgio dei Greci.*	w/c	
	190	*'A really good old Bit' at Chester.* (24 Albany Street.)	w/c	
1852	NWCS			
	9	*Chateau Crussol and Mont Pilate, near Valence on the Rhine.*	w/c	
	125	*The Old Post House in Carden, on the Moselle.*	w/c	
	226	*Abbeville, Rue des Changes.*	w/c	
	278	*Wildburg, near Treis, on the Moselle.*	w/c	

	280	*A Village Poorhouse.* (18 Albany Street.)	w/c			
1853	NWCS					
	12	*Walmer Castle, shewing the window* *of the Duke's chamber (the extreme* *on the left).* (18 Albany Street.)	w/c	11	11	0
1854	NWCS					
	25	*Havre du Port, Jersey.*	w/c	12	5	0
	35	*L'Islet in Boulay Bay, Jersey.*	w/c	6	16	6
	36	*Abbeville.*	w/c	17	10	0
	183	*Frankfort.*	w/c	17	10	0
	252	*Elizabeth Castle, Jersey.* (32 Albany Street.)	w/c	6	16	6
1854	Amateur Artists' Gallery, 121 Pall Mall.					
		Havre du Port, Jersey.	w/c	15	15	0
		Tour de Rozel from Boulay Bay, Jersey.	w/c	14	14	0
		St Aubin's Bay, Jersey.	w/c	12	12	0
		Elizabeth Castle, Jersey. (32 Albany Street.)	w/c	7	7	0
1855	NWCS					
	97	*A Sketch at Bournemouth.* (32 Albany Street.)	w/c	5	5	0
1856	NWCS					
	52	*London from Southwark Bridge.*	w/c	28	15	0
	75	*London from Southwark Bridge.*	w/c	28	15	6
	94	*Paris, from the Pont Royal.*	w/c	28	15	6
	127	*Roselle Bay, Jersey.*	w/c	25	0	0
	275	*St Aubin's Bay, Jersey.*	w/c	13	13	6
	293	*St Aubin's Bay, Jersey* (1st screen). (32 Albany Street.)	w/c	13	13	6
1857	NWCS					
	87	*The Porch to the Priory at Hampstead.* (66 Albany Street.)	w/c	5	5	0
1858	NWCS					
	42	*Leipzig.*	w/c	15	15	0
	318	*Old Bridge at Tournai.*	w/c	5	5	0
	330	*Ely Cathedral.* (66 Albany Street.)	w/c	5	5	0
1859	NWCS					
	49	*The Rath Haus, Prague.*	w/c			
	62	*Llan Egwest, or Valle Crucis Abbey,* *North Wales* (and verse 'I do love *these ancient ruynes*' etc.)	w/c	15	15	0

Year	Place and exhibition number	Title	Description	Price £ s d

Year	Place and exhibition number	Title	Description	£	s	d
	82	Crow Castle, or Dinas Bran, Llangollen (and verse 'The moon is up, and yet it is not night' etc.)	w/c	5	5	0
	184	Eliseg's Pillar, in the Vale of Crucis, near Llangollen.	w/c	5	5	0
	192	The Mardol, Shrewsbury.	w/c	31	10	0
	265	L'Hôtel de Ville, at the Hague.	w/c	15	15	0
	305	Old House, Little Moorfields, Chester.	w/c			
	307	Water Gate Tower, Chester.	w/c	3	3	0
	308	East End of Valle Crucis Abbey, Llangollen.	w/c	3	10	0
	324	The Phoenix, or King Charles's Tower, Chester.	w/c	3	3	0
	325	London from Greenwich Hill.	w/c	3	10	0
	327	Old Houses at Bourbon Lancy.	w/c	3	3	0
	328	The Tour de L'Horloge at St Fargeau.	w/c	3	3	0
	329	Valley Crucis from the Bran. (66 Albany Street.)	w/c	5	0	0
	Liverpool					
	728	The Rath-Haus, Prague.	w/c			
1860	NWCS					
	20	Remains of Old England—Worcester Friar Street looking towards Sidbury.	w/c	22	0	0
	47	Nuremburg.	w/c	17	5	0
	53	Porch to Shrewsbury Abbey Church.	w/c	3	3	0
	54	Remains of Old England—Market Hall, Shrewsbury.	w/c	22	0	0
	121	Remains of Old England—Friar Street, Worcester.	w/c	23	0	0
	139	Worcester Cathedral, east end.	w/c	17	0	0
	162	Remains of Old England—Old House in the High Street, Tewkesbury.	w/c	11	11	0
	230	Worcester, from St John's.	w/c	8	8	0
	267	The Bridge of Llangollen, looking towards Barber's Hill.	w/c	3	3	0
	268	Remains of the Parliament House of Owen Glendower, at Dolgelly.	w/c	3	3	0
	281	Remains of Old England—High Street, Salisbury.	w/c	27	0	0
	303	Llan Egwest, or Valley Crucis Abbey, in the Vale of Llangollen. (92 Albany Street.)	w/c	14	0	0
	Liverpool					
	10	Valle Crucis Abbey, Denbighshire.	w/c			
	36	High St. Shrewsbury. (92 Albany Street.)	w/c			

1861	NWCS						
	37	*The Church of St Laurent at Rouen.*	w/c	21	0	0
	106	*Old Towers at Prague—from the banks of the Moldaw.*	w/c	22	0	0
	260	*The Thein Kirche and Rathaus at Prague.* (92 Albany Street.)	w/c	21	0	0

	Liverpool						
	619	*Old Towers at Prague—from the Banks of the Moldaw.* (92 Albany Street.)	w/c			

1862	NWCS						
	1	*Silver Street, Salisbury.*	w/c	13	13	0
	14	*Hampton Court, from Mousley Lock.*	w/c	8	8	0
	49	*The King's Bridge at Prague.*	w/c	17	17	0
	120	*On the Thames at Richmond.*	w/c	4	4	0
	129	*Old House at Rouen.*	w/c	3	3	0
	132	*Eton College from the Thames.*	w/c	8	8	0
	154	*The Rathaus at Prague.*	w/c	21	0	0
	164	*On Lac Nemi, Roman States.*	w/c	3	13	6
	191	*Old Row in Watergate Street, Chester.*	w/c	5	5	0
	254	*Interior of Valle Crucis Abbey, looking West, Vale of Llangollen.*	w/c	13	13	0
	276	*The Vale of Llangollen, North Wales.* (92 Albany Street.)	w/c	11	0	0

	Liverpool						
	656	*Silver Street, Salisbury.* (34 Edward St., Hampstead Rd.)	w/c			

	International Exhibition						
	1367	*Amiens, from the banks of the Somme.* Owner: A.D. Smith Esq.	w/c			
	2691	*The Belfry at Ghent.*	chromo-lithograph			
	2692	*The Cathedral at Laon.* Owner: The Artist.	chromo-lithograph			

1863	NWCS						
	10	*The Old Hôtel de Ville of St Omer demolished in 1831.*	w/c	31	0	0
	179	*The Castle at Kranichstein, near Darmstadt; belonging to HRH The Grand Duke of Hesse Darmstadt. From a sketch by Mr Montague Cooke.*	w/c	9	0	0
	242	*Leipzig.*	w/c	16	10	0
	244	*Hesse Cassel.* (34 Edward Street.)	w/c	16	0	0

219

Year	Place and exhibition number	Title	Description	Price £ s d

Year	Place and exhibition number	Title	Description	£	s	d
1864	NWCS					
	22	*Nuremburg.*	w/c	31	10	0
	91	*The Old Castle at Oxford.*	w/c	13	13	0
	123	*Beauvais.*	w/c	31	10	0
	230	*Richmond Hill.*	w/c	37	10	0
		(34 Edward Street.)				
1865	NWCS					
	169	*East End of St Peter's Church, and Houses on the Bridge at Caen, Normandy.*	w/c			
	270	*On the Canal, Braunswig.*	w/c	20	0	0
	280	*The Apse of the Church of St Peter; and remains of the Old Chateau at Caen, Normandy.*	w/c	31	10	0
		(34 Edward Street.)				
1866	NWCS					
	1	*The Old Eschenheimer Tower and Gate at Francfort.*	w/c	15	0	0
	205	*The Old Hôtel de Ville at St Omer, demolished in 1831.*	w/c	30	0	0
	259	*The Old Porte de Bruxelles at Malines.*	w/c	5	5	0
	282	*The Castle and Mills at Oxford, from Bricknell's Meadow.*	w/c	8	0	0
		(34 Edward Street.)				
	NWCS (Winter)					
	40	*St Brelades Bay, Jersey.*	w/c	6	16	6
	54	*Entry to Plas Newydd, Llangollen.*	w/c	4	10	6
	72	*The Derby Palace, Chester—Walmer Castle.*	w/c	9	16	0
	91	*Westminster Abbey, Edward the Confessor's Chapel.*	w/c	21	10	0
	141	*Place du Grand Marché, Abbeville.*	w/c	20	10	0
	172	*The Rue des Juifs, Rouen.*	w/c	20	10	0
	210	*The Pont des Arts and l'Isle de la Cité, Paris—The Quai de la Concierge, Paris—The Bridge at Hampton Court.*	w/cs	20	8	0
	265	*Bishop Lloyds House at Chester.*	w/c	8	18	0
		Rock at Boulay Bay, Jersey.	w/c	8	10	6
	267	*The Slate Quarries near Newton Anner, Ireland.*	w/c	8	10	6
	301	*A Farmyard, Hatfield.*	w/c	7	10	6
	313	*At Bournemouth.*	w/c	4	10	6
	353	*Vale of Llangollen.*	w/c	8	10	0
	476	*Old Houses at Rouen.*	w/c	5	15	6
		(34 Edward Street.)				

1867	NWCS					
	174	*The Shambles, York.*	w/c	3	3	0
		(34 Edward Street.)				
	NWCS (Winter)					
	2	*Calais from the Marshes.*	w/c	12	12	0
	178	*A study, on a river's bank,*	w/c	8	8	0
		Twickenham, Surrey.	w/c	5	5	0
	228	*Cassel Hesse.*	w/c	21	0	0
	369	*Rue de la Tuile, Rouen.*	w/c	21	0	0
	412	*Norwich.*	w/c	12	12	0
		(15 King's College Rd., St. John's Wood.)				
1868	NWCS					
	169	*L'Hôtel de Ville, at Bethune.*	w/c	12	12	0
	178	*Rouen, The Church at St Laurent*				
		now used as a Depot for Diligences.	w/c	42	0	0
		(15 King's College Road.)				
	NWCS (Winter)					
	22	*The Tower at the Hôtel de Ville,*				
		at Bergnes.	w/c	21	0	0
	372	*The Hôtel de Ville at Vendome—*				
		Entry to the Palace at Gand, in which				
		was born Charles le Quint.	w/c	12	12	0
		(15 King's College Road.)				
1870	NWCS					
	84	*Le Chateau d'Amboise, on the Loire.*	w/c	47	5	0
	97	*Norwich Cathedral.*	w/c	12	12	0
	116	*South Porch of Shrewsbury Abbey Chirch.*	w/c	4	4	0
	117	*Entry to the Chateau Drie Torren, the*				
		house of David Teniers at Perck, near				
		Antwerp. The spread eagle on the gates was				
		painted by himself.	w/c	4	4	0
	131	*Ruins on a River's Bank.*	w/c	4	4	0
	134	*Entry to a house at the time of*				
		Francois I in the Rue des Marmousets,				
		Paris.	w/c	15	15	0
	250	*Abbeville (1st screen).*	w/c	15	15	0
		(King's College Road.)				
1871	NWCS (Winter)					
	122	*An old Tourelle on the Moselle.*	w/c	16	16	0
		(7 King's College Road.)				
1873	NWCS					
	95	*Market Day.*	w/c	15	15	0
		(7 King's College Road.)				

SELECT BIBLIOGRAPHY

Abbey, J. R.	*Scenery in Great Britain and Ireland in Aquatint and Lithography, 1770–1860,* London, 1952.
	Travel in Aquatint and Lithography, 1770–1860, 2 vols, London, 1956–57.
Barton, R.	'T. S. Boys, the Rowlandson of Victorian London', article in *The Antiquarian,* November 1931, pages 41–44.
Bénézit, E.	*Dictionnaire critique et documentaire des Peintres, Sculpteurs, Dessinateurs et Graveurs,* Vol. II, Paris, 1949, page 92.
Béraldi, H.	*Les Graveurs du XIXe siecle,* Vol. XII, Paris, 1892, pages 99–101.
Bryan, M.	*Biographical and critical dictionary of painters and engravers.* New edition, revised and enlarged, edited by K. E. Graves and W. Armstrong, 2 vols, London, 1893–95.
Burch, R. M.	*Colour Printing and Colour Printers,* London, 1910.
Burlington Fine Arts Club	*R. P. Bonington and his circle.* Exhibition catalogue, London, 1937.
Chancellor, E. B.	'A Great London Delineator, Thomas Shotter Boys', article in *The Connoisseur,* June 1921.
	'Boys in Paris', article in *The Architectural Review,* Vol. LX, 1926.
	Original Views of London as it is, by Thomas Shotter Boys, 1842, London, 1926.
	Disappearing London, London 1927
	Picturesque Architecture in Paris, Ghent, Antwerp, Rouen, etc., London, 1928.
	'A Recently Discovered Portrait of T. S. Boys', article in *Apollo,* Vol. XIV, 1931.
Cundall, H. M.	*William Callow Autobiography,* edited, London, 1908.
Dictionary of National Biography, London, 1886.	
Dubuisson, A. and Hughes, C. E.	*R. P. Bonington,* London, 1924.
Groschwitz, G. von	'T. S. Boys's London and Queen Victoria's etching', article in *Cincinnati Museum Bulletin,* December, 1952.
	'The Prints of T. S. Boys', essay in *Prints* by C. Zigrosser, London, 1963.
Hardie, M.	*English Coloured Books,* London, 1966.
	Water-colour Painting in Britain, 3 vols, London, 1967–69.
Ivins, W. M., Jnr.	'A Note on Some Old English Architectural Prints', article in *Bulletin of the Metropolitan Museum of Art,* New York, 1926.
Laver, J.	*Thomas Shotter Boys, Original Views of London,* 2 vols, Guildford, 1954–55.
Ottley, H.	*A Biographical and Critical Dictionary of Recent and Living Painters and Engravers,* London, 1866.
Stokes, H.	'Thomas Shotter Boys', article in *Walker's Quarterly,* No. 18, London, 1926.
Thieme, U. and Becker, F.	*Allgemeines Lexikon der Bildenden Kunstler,* Vol. IV, Leipzig, 1910, page 493.
Twyman, M. L.	*Lithography 1800–1850,* London, 1970.
Williams, I. O.	*Early English Watercolours,* London, 1952.

INDEX

Watercolours, prints and lithographs produced by Thomas Shotter Boys   *See also Appendix B*